THE EXCUSE DEPARTMENT IS CLOSED

HOW SMALL BUSINESS OWNERS AND SALES MANAGERS CAN ELIMINATE EXCUSES FOR NOT GETTING THE SALE

THOMAS MARTUCCI

ISBN: 978-1-6847-1213-7 (sc)
ISBN: 978-1-6847-1215-1 (hc)
ISBN: 978-1-6847-1214-4 (e)

Library of Congress Control Number: 2019916917

Lulu Publishing Services rev. date: 10/31/2019

CONTENTS

Section III

PREFACE

This book was written for two types of people: small business owners and sales managers who have just been promoted within small or midsize companies that provide little to no training.

If you are a small business owner, you have many different responsibilities, and time is not a luxury. This book will help you identify common excuses that can be prevented by having a better onboarding process for your sales team.

One common excuse is that most small business owners cannot afford to hire a professional sales training company. With this book, I will show you how to incorporate training into your regularly scheduled sales meetings. It gives you a heads up on some excuses that may indicate your sales team needs help.

Sales managers are often promoted because of their success in selling. Very rarely does the company provide formal education or training on how to be a successful sales manager, meaning that a sales manager is often in the same situation as the small business owner—facing lots of excuses. If you find yourself in this situation, this book is a resource to help you navigate them.

INTRODUCTION

Finding success as a small business owner is a bit like playing championship chess—if you don't know the lay of the board before making your opening gambit, your game can be lost before it's begun. The "game" of sales is beset with traps on every side—security breaches, lawsuits, maintaining a good reputation, and economic downturns. At times it seems virtually impossible to get ahead or even to stay afloat. For the most part, these external events can be countered, and the game can still be won. Internal factors, like closing deals, having enough leads to fill the sales funnel, and retaining qualified salespeople, are much more challenging. A guest speaker at the 2018 CEB Marketing Leadership Council Conference outlined some frightening statistics:

- The average tenure of a salesperson is less than two years[1]
- The average tenure of a sales manager is nineteen months
- 67 percent of companies say it takes seven months or more for new salesperson to become fully productive (47 percent say it takes ten months or more)[2]

In September 2018, *Forbes Magazine* reported that 57 percent of sales reps do not meet their quotas, according to Salesforce's third annual "State of Sales" report. Though this is troubling news for any company, it can spell defeat for a small business owner.

Your sales force is the lifeblood of your company and one of the most difficult, if not the hardest, sectors to hire for. Before it pays off, it requires the largest investment of time and money, which can greatly stress small operations. Regardless of their previous experiences or backgrounds, for you to achieve peak success your team members will

---

[1] Sales Readiness Group
[2] CSO Insights

need training on your product(s), service(s), and internal operations. However, most small business I have encountered, including my own, may not have the resources to hire a sales training company.

Not unlike the way a human heart needs blood, without a continuous flow of sales, a company will inevitably wither and die. It is therefore imperative that a sales manager or small business owner be vigilant over the sales process and well prepared to provide his or her sales force with the tools it needs to close the sale.

I write this book from two perspectives—first, from that of a division president and sales manager of a large public company who took a division from zero to $50 million in the consumer product industry in less than eight years, and second, from that of a small business owner who started a company from nothing and took in $18 million.

After coming off active duty with the military, my first selling position was with Dial Soap in the metro Albany, New York, area. My immediate manager told me if I didn't get a promotion within two years then I should start looking for another job. So, heeding his advice, I joined GAF Corporation selling film and cameras in the upstate New York and Vermont territories. This was my first encounter with how a midsize company (GAF had about $200 million in sales) could operate with no onboarding procedure. The national sales manager who hired me handed me a list of accounts and told me that a car was waiting for me in New Jersey. I didn't hear from him for two weeks.

From there, I was promoted to district sales manager in the Northeast and subsequently national accounts specializing in the catalog showroom industry (selling to companies like Best Products and Service Merchandise). Within a year and half, GAF decided to close the camera and film division. There I was, twenty-eight years old, having just moved to the metro New York area with a wife and two-year-old, and now I had no job.

As I started to interview, I realized that the same thing could happen again with another company. I decided right then to start my own business as an independent sales rep working on commissions, specializing in the catalog showroom industry. I sold consumer products from cameras to giftware to electronics to luggage. That was when I first realized how unprepared small businesses were to provide the tools, information, and training necessary to sell their products. I had to develop my own procedures, finding answers to buyers' objections as I went along.

I had a great run for twelve years, but I knew it was going to fade away, which it did in 1992. A few years earlier, I'd sold one of my better companies that had started from zero and was at that point doing $5 million in annual sales. The new ownership asked if I'd really earned this much commission the previous year, and I said yes. As I knew my time representing that company was short. I approached my major accounts and asked whether they would buy from me if I could bring in a line as good as or better. They agreed.

That began my foray into designing and making luggage in Asia for retailers under their names. I also made cases for the cellular phone industry and medical diabetes cases. When the catalog industry went away, my new company took up where it left off. I did this for ten years, but I got tired of carrying inventory and the problems associated with it. I was also getting a lot of excuses from my sales team of independent sales reps who made commissions when they sold something. I sold to retailers like Walmart, Target, department stores, and drugstore chains.

After liquidating and selling the business, I started to consult for a variety of companies. One company wanted me to set up and run their luggage division, which seemed interesting because they were a $2 billion public company in the clothing industry. So, I started their luggage division; the brand was Calvin Klein. Their onboarding process was the worst I had ever seen. They didn't know anything about the luggage industry and wouldn't admit it. But with my help, in eight years we took it from zero to over $50 million.

Having spent most of my adult life in sales and small business, I have heard and seen just about every excuse. I realized that many of these problems could have been resolved by a much better onboarding process and regular informal coaching. Now I am trying to help small businesses and sales managers overcome obstacles and give them some insights. The first venture is this book.

Some excuses indicate that salespeople may be in the wrong profession or company. Other excuses seek to justify why a sales force is unable to get an order, make a sale, or meet a sales budget goal. In my own roles, I would often find myself saying to members of my team, "You have an excuse to fit every situation." Though many of these excuses were funny the first time I heard them, I found myself questioning whether a given salesperson was a good fit for my team after receiving the same ones on a regular basis. These excuses quickly become frustrating and stressful because the success of your company lies directly upon your shoulders, and you can't walk every salesperson through every assignment. As business philosopher Jim Rohn said, "If you really want to do something, you will find a way. If you don't, you will find an excuse." Upon considering these words, I decided to take preemptive measures to identify the most common excuses my team might use, consider their perspectives, and find a solution to address them.

Once, one of my sales team members returned to the office after an unsuccessful sales presentation and gave me an excuse for not getting the order. I empathized because the week prior, I had been running late from a meeting and rushed my presentation when I should have rescheduled it. When I first started out in sales, after each call, I would do an "after-action analysis"—a process I learned in the military. It involved retracing my steps to determine what went well, what did not, and how to best improve future presentations from what I learned. I shared this experience with my salesperson, and it inspired me to think beyond the excuse itself. Maybe some critical elements were missing in our "sales toolbox," ones I should have provided to my team.

As I pondered this, I considered each excuse and the response I gave; I also considered discussions I'd had with fellow sales managers. I began to recognize patterns, and I categorized them into the following problem areas:

a) Tools or training that the salesperson did not have
b) Missing information or a misunderstanding of the product, service, industry, or company
c) A poor fit for the sales team, a lack of drive, or an unwillingness to do the work assigned

Addressing the first two areas was my responsibility as sales manager and became increasingly more so when I became a small business owner. The third was also my responsibility but could also be attributed to issues with screening and hiring. Generally, there is no salesperson that knows more about a product or company than its sales manager or small business owner. When taking all this into consideration, I came to believe that in order to separate my successful team members from my less successful, I had to remove the first two types of excuses for not completing a sale and then determine whether a lack of sales was due to a coachable fault or if it was grounds for dismissal.

In the following pages, we will dissect a variety of excuses for not making a sale that I have heard over my thirty years of experience. Section 1 focuses on the first type of excuses—those related to training or tools that an employee may not have; section 2 highlights excuses that stem for not understanding important information about the product, company, or industry; and the excuses in section 3 are often a result of poor employee motivation or fit for the profession.

This book is intended to help you understand the mentality of your sales force, evaluate excuses that employees may have, determine whether they are based in reality, and explore opportunities for retraining or coaching. As the leadership of sales management, your role in preventing the loss of future sales is to provide support, good counsel, and redirection as appropriate. I hope the experience I share here will provide you with the tools to do so.

SECTION I

Excuses in section 1 arise when your employees are unfamiliar with the good, the bad, and the ugly of your company's policies and procedures. These fundamentals should be reviewed with your sales team during the onboarding process. It is always better for the sales team to hear about any issues from you rather than a customer or prospective customer. It gives salespeople the ability to discuss your company's policies and procedures with the customer or prospective customer without having to come back to you looking for the answers.

I suggest that you build an onboarding manual for your sales team to encourage efficiency among newly hired sales team members.

Sales is the oxygen in your business blood stream.
—*Thomas Martucci*

EXCUSE 1
My Leads Aren't Leads!

I have participated in many trade and consumer shows in the United States and around the world and always encounter the same problem: I get a lead, but it seems to evaporate into thin air almost immediately after the show ends. I have confronted this problem at every level: as a salesperson, as a sales manager, and as a small business owner. It never ceases to be frustrating. The most common reasons leads fizzle out are incorrect contact information, a buyer who was looking for a personal product purchase, and being unable to contact the person with whom I was directed to discuss my product.

I have attempted to conduct research on what percentage of leads become valid. As it turns out, it is a hard thing to calculate. I reached out to my colleagues as well as my sales team to ask if they knew what percentage of their leads becomes valid, what percentage of leads goes into the sales funnel, and what percentage becomes a client or customer. The reaction I got nine times out of ten was a shrug of the shoulders. It should be noted that, other than the members of my sales team, all these people were small business owners who did not have the money, personnel, or resources to have a robust CRM program or full-time marketing department.

As I looked further into how my colleagues processed leads, I found the answer often was that they didn't. When I asked them if they had a formal or informal lead-processing plan, the answer was usually either a resounding no at worst or a somewhat informal plan at best. This surprised me greatly, especially when I thought of how much money one stands to lose at a trade show with poor planning.

Participating in a trade show can cost anywhere from $10,000 to $50,000, and a consumer table show can cost between $3,000 and $5,000. E&E Exhibit Solutions says you can estimate your total event budget by multiplying the cost of your space by three. For example, the average floor space costs $21 per square foot, so for a 20×20 floor space rental, you can expect to pay around $8,400. The budget for that event would then be approximately $25,200. As a result, I was compelled to determine my ROI on these trade shows and develop a lead-processing plan.

There are many ways to gain leads at a trade show, but there is no guarantee that they are valid. Additionally, it is easy in such a busy setting to either lose contact information or obtain incorrect information. For example, like many companies, we would go to these shows and use a swipe machine to capture lead info. Though this was easy, it was not very useful because the name on the badge you swipe may not be the person you are talking with.

Note-taking is a separate process. Where do you put the notes you took for that meeting? Because these conversations are rarely recorded, it is highly likely these notes will get lost or mixed with other contact information. To resolve these issues, my team decided to use the old-school process of developing a lead sheet, which can be found on the next page. This would vary from show to show based on the objectives of that show. According to Brook Salomon, director at Dell Global Alliance Events, the industry average for time spent in a booth is about seven minutes. Knowing this, tailor your list carefully, allowing for natural conversation as opposed to a survey.

Example of a Trade Show Lead Sheet

Name of Show		
Dates of Show		

Date: _____		Company Employee: _____

Customer Name: _____		
Address: _____		
		business card
City: _____		
Country: _____		

Type of Account:
Retailer: _____ # of Stores/Locations: _____
Importer: _____
Distributor: _____ County/Countries: _____
Factory: _____ Type of Factory: _____

Comment/Discussion:
_____
_____
_____
_____
_____
_____
_____
_____
_____
_____
_____
_____
_____
_____
_____
_____
_____
_____

Assessment and Follow Up: What is Potential A   B   C   Other/Expalin
_____
Date to Follow Up
_____
Who ios assigned the follow up
_____

10/31/2019C:\Users\Tfabricante.ASI\AppData\Local\Microsoft\Windows\INetCache\Content.Outlook\4OIZXSST\Nameof Show

Business cards are the single most important element of a solid lead sheet. It is rare for any participant to come without them. This will provide you with a name and necessary contact information. After a prospect leaves, staple or tape the business card to the lead sheet.

My team and I wanted a lead sheet prepared for customers of all sizes. This took convincing the sales team and a bit of tough love, but it has since proven to be a very effective tool.

We began holding a team meeting approximately one week before the trade show to review our objectives. We found that one of our problems was with our dependence on computers. Very few, if any, orders are written at trade shows, but we agreed to remain willing to take them if necessary.

In reviewing our process, we discovered lead sheet control was a problem because many salespeople who worked leads at trade shows mixed them in with their personal belongings. In our preshow meetings, we discussed the importance of the lead sheets and why we wanted them collected in one place. The primary reason was to have two people review the sheets at the end of the day or during a lull in the show. They would review the sheets as if they were going to do the follow-up. If they had questions, they could easily go to the person who wrote the sheet and get clarification. This was critical because recalling a discussion two or three hours after the show is so much easier and more fruitful than three or four days later.

At the end of each day at a show, we would meet and review each sheet filled out that day, regardless of whether it was a lead or current customer. Whoever prepared the sheet would give a verbal recap of the meeting without looking at the sheet. You would be surprised how much more information we gleaned and documented from their verbal recaps.

We now had a list of leads that was tremendously better than those from the past. Instituting this process greatly reduced the excuse "The leads I get are not real leads." Our current system can now track leads, as we developed a simple Excel tracking system by show and by salesperson that we can reference during our monthly sales review. Since its development, I've received fewer excuses and have been able to calculate the ROI on shows while also obtaining good insight on the ability of the salesperson to close.

In order to improve the process for a small company with limited resources, it is crucial to keep track of leads, improve sales, and reduce duplication. Every owner's process will need to be shaped to suit his or her needs best, but the essentials should be the same. By ensuring that your sales teams are using the same tracking procedures and tools, keeping lead sheets centralized, and meeting regularly to discuss these leads, you will be more organized and successful.

Teamwork is the ability to work together toward a common vision. The ability to direct individual accomplishments toward organizational objectives. It is the fuel that allows common people to attain uncommon results.

—*Andrew Carnegie*

Customers Find Our Quality Standards Unacceptable

Almost every, if not all, sales manager and small business owner has been confronted with the serious concern that a perspective customer is not satisfied with the quality of a product. It is easy, upon hearing such complaints, to have an emotionally charged reaction and to blame the salesperson for the issue. The appropriate response, however, is to assess the situation, discuss the matter with the salesperson, determine why he or she thinks the customer is dissatisfied with the quality, and find a resolution to the issue. A cooler head allows you to ease the mind of the salesperson and put him or her in a better position to offer solutions to rescue the sale. An angry reaction is not productive and puts your salesperson on the defense, and the sale remains lost.

If you receive this excuse from your customers via your salesperson, you must determine the validity of the customers' concerns. If there have not been preexisting problems, now is the time to gather your sales force, have a frank discussion, and develop a quality-review process. It could be that this is an invitation to improve the quality of your product or service, which may in turn improve sales across the board.

What Is Quality?

The business dictionary defines quality as follows:

> a measure of excellence, or a state of being free from defects, deficiencies, or significant variations, which is attained by strict and consistent commitment to certain standards that bring about uniformity of a product in order to satisfy specific customer requirements.

Alternatively, according to the International Organization for Standardization, quality is defined as the totality of features and characteristics of a product or service that bears its ability to satisfy stated or implied needs. Ultimately, the goal of your sales team is to ensure that potential customers trust the company and the quality of its products to successfully close a sale. There are many approaches one can take, but the following should be considered:

1. **Make your customers feel heard. Listen up!**

    In many scenarios, customers do not want immediate solutions to their complaints as much as they want the assurance they are heard and given consideration. Attempting to provide immediate rebuttals or solutions to customers without first hearing what they have to say could be interpreted as being told they are wrong or being placated, and that may further agitate them.

    For example, when a customer has a quality concern, the following rebuttal is not productive: "I suggest you check properly, as our products are always of high quality."

    This reply does not address the concern, feels dismissive to the customer, and will likely not end in a successful sale.

    A more appropriate response would be to reflect the feelings the customer is having back to them and to repeat what was heard. Here is an example:

    > It must have been inconvenient for you to have purchased our product, only to find out that it doesn't meet your quality expectations. We are truly sorry that you had this experience and would like to help resolve your concerns. Can you tell us more about it?

    This response opens a door for communication, indicates that the salespeople are willing to hear what they have been told, demonstrates that they understand why the customers are unsatisfied, and presents opportunities for resolution.

2. **Train your employees, and teach them to listen!**

A little bit of employee training goes a long way in reshaping the way customers see your product, thereby influencing the way the quality of your product is assessed. In top business organizations, training is an essential aspect of an employee enhancement program. Training sessions and workshops improve the skill set of your employees while helping them adapt to new technologies and stay competent in their respective fields.

In small businesses, training sessions and workshops are not always logistically or economically feasible; in such circumstances an exchange of experiences and ideas amongst the sales team is the best way to encourage conversations about quality. In my own experience, I learned about quality by selling and manufacturing for large companies in the medical and automobile industries, both of which had very rigid quality standards. To ensure these standards were met, I developed systems and processes that I was later able to share with my sales team.

I taught or demonstrated to my salespeople the key quality issues of the products, as well as our quality assurance (QA) processes. This instruction was usually done as on-the-job training in real time on a sales presentation in front of a buyer. Sometimes, a buyer would ask me about the quality of our product compared to competitors, but I would only discuss it if asked. I enjoyed the fact that I knew the difference.

When I made a presentation on products, I would always discuss quality and clearly demonstrate the ends we went to, to ensure quality was up to standards. I would always end the presentation by explaining that we knew all products are not 100 percent perfect and that we developed the Plan-Do-Check-Act (PDCA) cycle to continuously improve our quality. After shadowing one of these presentations, my sales team members understood our QA process, saw that this was no longer an acceptable excuse, and had a resolution to enact themselves.

Because I took a confident, thoughtful, and thorough approach to each presentation, most of my buyers never questioned the quality of my products and often asked my opinions about other quality concerns they faced, which was not only gratifying but indicative of their trust in my product or service. Teaching this approach to my sales force gave them an invaluable tool that they could customize to their own needs and find success with. It required no extra expenditure of money on the part of the company and provided the sales team with the training they needed to accomplish their goals.

No matter how you accomplish it, as a sales manager you should strive to integrate an employee training program into the business structure. Lead by example.

3. **Insist on continuous improvement**

Improvements must be continuous to consistently meet your customers' quality expectations. As the famous adage goes, "There is always room for improvement." In your role a sales manager, you should continually strive to be at the top of your game when it comes to delivering quality products and services, which brings us to the need for a better understanding of the Plan-Do-Check-Act (PDCA) cycle.

The PDCA cycle involves searching for possible areas where improvement is necessary followed by making the appropriate changes. Then, you should regularly check to see the impact that these changes have on product quality to see if the improvement was successful. If improvement is achieved, the cycle is completed with acting, wherein you implement the same improvement pattern across other needed areas.

If you have not incorporated a company-wide QA process, there is nothing for your sales team to report during a sales presentation and no way to assure a potential customer of your quality standards. If this is the case, a QA process should be immediately implemented and reported to the sales team. After all, they cannot be expected to come fully prepared to a presentation unless necessary details are available to them.

It may be discouraging and frustrating to hear that a potential client finds your quality standards unacceptable, even more so when it's communicated indirectly through your sales team. Instead of looking at it as a failure to make a sale, however, reframe the issue as an opportunity for change, growth, and, potentially, greater success. Listen to your client. Listen to your staff. Teach where appropriate, and learn where you can.

Profit in business comes from repeat customers, customers that boast about your product, your quality and service, and that bring friends with them.
—*W. Edwards Deming*

The Customer Had a Negative Previous Experience

As a sales manager or small business owner, you know that complaints from your customers are to be expected. Their feedback should compel you to examine your workflow processes, evaluate your customer service model and how it is carried out by your staff, and upgrade your products if necessary. One of many possible complaints could be that a customer had a bad experience with your company, possibly years ago. These negative experiences can carry as much weight as positive ones in determining whether a customer will give you repeat business—perhaps even more. Both are memorable, but a negative experience is more likely to be recalled. You are then challenged to reframe that experience into a positive one, if possible. The onus falls upon you to assure customers that their feedback has been taken into consideration and that you have taken steps to allay their concerns.

It is also your responsibility to prepare your sales force for a customer who has had a negative experience. Was the issue corrected or resolved? Was the customer satisfied with the results? The most effective salesperson on your team will be the one who can de-escalate a hostile situation, provide reassurance, and maintain a clear line of communication between themselves, their client, and the management.

I recommend the following suggestions for optimizing a positive customer experience while addressing a customer's concerns:

1. **Listen to your customer**

   Encourage the salesperson to be a proactive listener. Before beginning the presentation, he or she should check in with you're the client about any outstanding issues or concerns. Some may consider this a somewhat controversial approach, but I have found that providing my customers with an opportunity to speak about their experiences—good or bad—listening closely, and responding with genuine concern allowed them to be more receptive to what I had to say. Without the distraction of their previous negative experience at the forefront of their minds, they are much more attentive and easier to engage.

Your salesperson must also be an active listener, giving customers space to express their concerns without interruption or an immediate response. I believe, and have tried to train my salespeople, that "the good Lord gave you two eyes, two ears, and one mouth, so look and listen twice as much as you talk."

Another saying, "the customers are always right," is also one that a good businessperson keeps in mind. A salesperson should show clients that they're being heard by asking open-ended questions to draw out their concerns and to reflect what he or she understands. For example: "You say you had a bad experience with us a few years ago—can you tell me more about that?" When they respond, your salesperson might reply with, "It sounds like that was very frustrating. What can we do to improve your interactions with us?" Sometimes being heard is all that is necessary, and the salesperson may then proceed with the transaction.

2. **Go on the defense without being defensive**

Upon hearing what the customer has had to say, your salesperson may be tempted to take an argumentative or defensive strategy to prove that a negative experience was not your company's fault. A customer may tell your salesperson something he or she does not want to hear, does not agree with, or finds offensive. Instead of being argumentative, your salesperson should respond to the customer's concerns, demonstrating how your company resolved them, be it through a new standard of products, new staffing, or other improvement. This will assure them that they can trust the salesperson with an honest opinion and that steps have already been taken to remedy the problem.

3. **Assure your customer with a sample or presentation**

Everyone loves free samples. To foster trust and confidence in your service and products, you may want your salespeople to consider sending a customer a complimentary sample of your product. The intent here is to demonstrate the improved quality of your product and allow customers to see it for themselves. If they had a negative experience in the past, this may help them to see the evolution of your product line since that time.

A presentation may also be in order. Here, the salesperson should arrange to have enough time to present new products, verify their new quality, explain what makes the current product better than the previous ones, and allow the customer to see the product in action.

4. **Keep the lines of communication open**

A good salesperson is one who can impress customers and hold their attention with both attitude and words. However, it is very possible that even after the salesperson has gone through all the steps, the customer is still not satisfied. It could be that he or she is not convinced or does not see acceptable improvements. In these situations, your salesperson can only assure that customer of further improvement. The salesperson should affirm how important the customer's feedback is and what will be done with it so that customer is confident all complaints will be relayed to the appropriate leadership and that action will be taken.

5. **Communicate your expectations about customer relations to your staff**

As a sales manager, you are acutely aware of the value of the customer-sales force relationship. It drives the success of your business and determines the number of customers you can both attract and retain. Because selling requires a great deal of conversation, misunderstandings can easily occur. For example, profanity, a poorly timed or inappropriate joke, or personal questions can quickly destroy a positive business relationship. For this reason, as a sales manager or small business owner you should be observant of how your sales force communicates with customers, clearly define what is and is not appropriate for the workplace, and provide feedback and counseling to staff as appropriate. These issues should be resolved in real time so immediate action and repair of relationships can occur.

With effort, a willingness to improve, and openness to criticism, it is possible to improve customer relations and bring customers back into the fold. In addition to seeking opportunities to improve, also explore opportunities for recognition. Your sales team should encourage customers to share their positive experiences with colleagues or friends to expand your client base. The combination of process improvement and good customer service will ensure your company's future success.

The harder the conflict, the more glorious the triumph
—*Thomas Paine*

I Had Interference from an Associate

During a sales presentation, a salesperson may find it useful to call in reinforcements like a product manager, a technology expert, or a more experienced team member to provide additional information, answer questions, demonstrate a product, or provide mentorship. But this person may take up too much time in a presentation, a potential buyer may not like the person, or the information the associate provides may not be particularly useful. Though your salesperson may have had a clearly delineated, planned presentation, these types of things typically go awry at the last minute. It is also tricky to coach a salesperson through these circumstances; you may not be the direct supervisor of the consulting associate, so you and the salesperson may have limited control over what occurs. If you find yourself in this situation, you must focus on the salesperson's efforts and concerns. Here is how to address a rogue associate who may be taking over a presentation:

1. **Determine why the associate was consulted**

    Did the associate need to be there? Could another sales team member have been consulted instead? Asking your salesperson about the purpose of the associate's involvement may help determine how this could better be handled in future situations.

2. **Instruct a salesperson to ask associates what they will present beforehand**

    Your sales team member should ask the person invite to speak what he or she intends to say and then verify that it is appropriate, on topic, and interesting. If the salesperson does not agree with what is planned, encourage immediate feedback, asking the speaker to edit part of the presentation or, if it continues to be problematic, requesting the speaker not to attend at all. Though it is ideal for a potential buyer to be able to have any questions or concerns about a product addressed directly by someone with more knowledge or experience, it is not worth losing a sale to include associates who are problematic.

3. **Suggest a salesperson designate a time limit for the associate to speak**

Urge your salesperson to set a specific time limit for any auxiliary speaker during a presentation, to communicate this time limit clearly beforehand, and to remind the associate not to exceed it. If, during a presentation, the speaker does not respect the time constraint, the salesperson should take the initiative, respectfully thank the associate for his or her time, and continue with the rest of the presentation. Getting the presentation back on track is well worth a moment of awkwardness.

4. **In the future, suggest the salesperson do a "dress rehearsal" with the speaker before a presentation**

This practice session does not necessarily have to include a full or formal presentation; just meeting to discuss its flow will establish your salesperson as the leader. Here, expectations can be discussed, potential conflicts or concerns can be addressed, and any requirements for audiovisual or demonstration materials can be determined. If possible, it may be helpful to have your salesperson preview the presentation with another colleague to solicit feedback—the colleague may see something the sales member does not.

5. **Ensure your salesperson introduced the invited guest and explained his or her role**

   A potential buyer might be confused about why a salesperson has invited additional presenters. At the beginning of the meeting, the salesperson should introduce any guests and their roles in the presentation. Then the buyer can listen to what the guests have to say and can move forward.

6. **Instruct your salesperson to follow the buyer's cues**

   During the presentation, a good salesperson should be watching his or her audience for cues, paying particularly close attention when a guest speaks. Instruct your sales staff to watch for signs of boredom, annoyance, and engagement and to respond quickly and appropriately.

7. **Instruct your salesperson to provide the speaker with visual cues**

   Sometimes speakers are unaware that they have exceeded their allotted time. Subtle visual cues, including eye contact or tapping on a wrist to indicate their time is up, are useful to help wrap up in a timely fashion.

An auxiliary speaker can be an excellent resource, but this person can also invite an element of unpredictability into a well-rehearsed presentation. By managing expectations early, setting clear boundaries, and observing how a buyer responds, a salesperson has a good chance of maintaining control of the presentation.

Unity is strength. When there is teamwork and collaboration, wonderful things can be achieved.
—*Mattie Stepanek*

My Territory Is Too Large or Too Small

I'm sure you're familiar with the story "Goldilocks and the Three Bears" and how Goldilocks searched for the chair, the porridge, and the bed that were just right. Much like the curly-haired heroine of that story, salespeople are often in search of the territory that is just right for them. For some, a territory may be too large and too difficult to manage alone. For others, a territory may be too small, without enough clientele to develop a strong client base. But enlarging smaller territories or restricting activities in larger ones may present problems for customers, as they may lose specialized attention or be cut out of a sales area, which may, in turn, hurt business. Thus, territory size can be a source of continual frustration for both you and your sales force. Here, I discuss how to address territory size and how to discuss this issue with your sales force.

Before making decisions about resizing a territory, you must ask yourself several questions:

1) Have you researched the sales needs of this territory?
2) Do you know the number of potential accounts or expected volume in this territory?
3) Do you have an idea of the optimum number of accounts, the cycle of seeing accounts, and the sales volume one salesperson can handle per specific territory?

The salesperson's feeling that a territory is either too big or too small will vary from person to person. A salesperson with a small territory may want a larger one to increase sales, while one with a larger territory may want to increase effectiveness by reducing the territory. The solution for each scenario will differ with each salesperson and is unlikely to be uniform.

Options for addressing concerns regarding a large territory may include the following:

1. **Reduce the size of the territory—trim the fat**

   A salesperson with too large a territory may feel overextended despite his or her best efforts. The easiest solution may be to reduce the size of the territory. Test with a smaller territory and observe your sales member's performance. If it improves, you have found a size that will optimize results. If no improvement is observed, continue reducing the size of the territory until sales do improve.

2. **Add another salesperson—many hands make light work**

   The addition of second salesperson to a territory is another excellent solution. He or she can assist with the distribution of goods or be assigned specific customers, thus enabling your team to cover more ground and perhaps expand the territory.

3. **Provide logistical support—getting there is half the job!**

   Providing a means of transportation to your salesperson could be all the support needed. A means of transportation will not only ensure he or she covers more territory but will also decrease the time it takes to do that.

The problem with these solutions, however, is that they all increase your sales costs. Before adding a new salesperson, you should determine both the incremental cost and the incremental sales expected from the change. For example, I was a sales manager for both the New York and New England territories and had one salesperson covering upstate New York and Vermont. He complained that the territory was too large.

I conducted a study on the territory, the accounts, and the volume expectations and realized that there was a lot of driving between the account sites. We were able to transfer the eastern Vermont territory to the salesperson overseeing Maine and New Hampshire. At the same time, I transferred the western New York territory to the salesperson overseeing Ohio and Western Pennsylvania. I developed a new sales budget and account list for each salesperson and was confident that the adjustments were beneficial for everyone involved. As a result, my sales force performed better and experienced better job satisfaction, and we also saw an incremental increase in sales.

Options for addressing concerns regarding a small territory include the following:

1. **Increase the territory—give them some space to roam!**

   Your salesperson may have covered most of his or her territory and is looking for more. You need people like this in your business, for they will earn you more sales when provided with places to reach. This may also be an opportunity to exchange the salesperson's territory place with someone who complains about having a territory that is too large. In the long run, the person who says a territory is too small is likely to serve you well and be a good fit in a larger territory. Provide them the opportunity and monitor his or her progress.

2. **Motivate the salesperson—think beyond the carrot on the stick**

   A salesperson may feel he or she is not performing up to his or her capacity and ask for a larger territory. This person is clearly motivated and should be supported to stay that way. You should encourage this attitude. This kind of energy is infectious and may inspire other members of your sales force. Providing larger or more territories to a person like this will provide further motivation, which could lead to promotions, an increase in salary, and keeping the salesperson engaged and productive.

3. **Transfer territories—a change of scenery can be good!**

    Changing locations is inevitable if you cannot enlarge a salesperson's current territory. You are likely aware of locations that are more demanding, as well as their opportunities and challenges and how they correspond with the strengths and weaknesses of the salespeople overseeing them.

When considering personnel moves, you must be intimately familiar with your territories, and you must know your staff and your expectations about how each salesperson should perform in each area. Keeping an open line of communication with your team will enable all to perform at their best, reach their goals, and optimize your results.

If you do not have a defined process that moves your people forward so they can achieve greater results, then what is it you are managing?

—*Keith Rosen*

My Sales Quota Is Too High

Setting expectations of your sales team can be a tricky tightrope to walk. There is a fine line between setting them too low, which can lead to complacency, and setting them so high that they feel unattainable. In general, good salespeople are driven and optimistic, with a healthy dose of competitiveness. When a goal is set for such salespeople, they will do everything in their power not only to meet it but to exceed it. There are times, however, even in the best careers, where salespeople cannot meet their sales quota, which they then often consider too high. An immediate fix to this situation may not exist, but an honest conversation, an exploration of potential barriers, and reassurance that this will not threaten his or her job are all steps in a positive direction to getting back on track. Several tactics can be used here:

1. **Examine current conditions**

   Consider what is happening in the market. Are other sales team members experiencing similar difficulties? Are your competitors? There may be factors that cannot be accounted for by numbers alone. Get a feel for the landscape before drawing conclusions.

2. **Review past performance**

   Look at historical statistics. Look for trends. Have these drops in sales happened before? Did performance drop at specific times or for known reasons, and are circumstances similar now? If so, you and your salesperson can identify these issues and discuss them, finding a course of action to prevent them in the future.

Look at both historical highs and lows and discuss what was happening when things were going well. If no trends are found, now is a good time to begin tracking this information so you have the data ready in the future. Ideally, this should be a tool to benefit you both, as opposed to calling out previous failures.

3. **Do not make this discussion adversarial**

   Your salesperson very likely knows things aren't going well, and knowing one's performance is poor is not good for morale. Do not add to this person's angst by making the discussion a "management versus sales team" scenario. Instead, approach it with compassion and empathy—those of us who have been in sales know what a rough patch feels like. This does not mean, however, that you can or should be permissive of poor performance if there is no indication that the salesperson intends to correct his or her course.

4. **Discuss internal and external factors**

   Factors affecting performance that you are not aware of may be at play. Engage your team member in a friendly conversation about his or her family, what he or she does with free time, and how he or she maintains work-life balance. By listening attentively, you may be able to pick up some hints about outside factors or stressors at work. Feel free to discuss opportunities for self-care (e.g., taking time off or reducing work hours).

5. **Involve your sales team in quota development**

   Again, good salespeople are driven and competitive. Therefore, how they respond to a reasonable quota should be a reliable gauge for how well they will perform. If the quota is too low, they may become disinterested and less inclined to push themselves. If the quota is too high, they may psych themselves out. They know what they are capable of, as do you. Present them with the data you have used to develop quotas so they understand how and why you came to that conclusion. Do this on a regular basis to maintain transparency. Negotiating a quota together will not only ensure it is attainable, but it will give each salesperson a feeling of autonomy and empowerment.

6. **Understand that not every salesperson will respond well to the same approach**

One of the most important factors for engaging in these types of conversations is acknowledging that every member of your team is an individual, and each will have a very different philosophy and approach to sales. When developing action plans, discuss motivators, incentives, and how they would like to be recognized for their efforts. These will vary greatly; taking a "cookie cutter" approach will be an exercise in futility. Consider your sales team your "internal customers" with the understanding that, like buyers, they have preferences, opinions, and boundaries. When they feel heard and respected, they will be more amenable to hear what you have to say in return.

7. **Develop an action plan together**

By combining historical data and your goals with those of your salesperson, the outline for an action plan should come together quite easily. Discuss goals, what success might look like, where improvements can or should be made, and the timeframes or deadlines in which they should be completed.

8. **Develop a reporting system**

You may need more data. Consider developing an interim reporting system to track the initial results of your action plan. Here, have your salesperson record intended goals, his or her progress toward those goals, potential barriers, and goals for the following reporting period. This will be a tool that you both may use to view progress and anticipate future successes and challenges.

9. **Agree upon an incentive**

    It bears repeating that every salesperson is an individual, with differing preferences about incentives. Ask your team member how he or she would like to see efforts rewarded. Discuss whether those incentives are possible and the terms for how and when this might occur (e.g., annually or quarterly). Upon successful negotiation, document the agreement.

10. **Get to work!**

    There is nothing that can't be accomplished with honesty, courtesy, and clearly delineated expectations. Understanding that for every success there is a challenge, we remind ourselves that we are human and are prone to mistakes and imperfections. A good sales manager or small business owner recognizes this. A great one is willing to collaboratively work on it to benefit all.

There are no traffic jams along the extra mile.
                                                    —*Roger Staubach*

EXCUSE 7

My Buyer Wants Guaranteed Sales

Sales will always include a bit of a gamble. You can't predict uncontrollable factors like trends, product inventories, or the economy. Though salespeople may want to guarantee with absolute certainty that their buyers will be successful in reselling their products, it simply cannot be done. It is a fool's errand to guarantee sales to a potential buyer—ultimately, it will return to haunt you. Instead, it is better to manage a client's expectations early in the negotiation process to prevent any potential surprises, miscommunications, or anger. Though this excuse is one of the more understandable ones, you would be wise to address it quickly, especially if the salesperson giving it is new to the company. In fact, incorporating a company-wide policy about making guarantees should be considered. Below are some suggestions for how to best negotiate making a guarantee to a potential buyer:

1. **Arm your salespeople with facts**

   Provide your sales team and any potential buyers up front with as much information as possible about how well a product sells. You can do this by sharing results from other clients, from your competition, or from national or international averages. Share examples of contracts or positive reviews from previous clients to demonstrate your company's ability to get the results your clients seek.

2. **Determine whether a guarantee is necessary**

   It may be that a product does not require a guarantee. Encourage your salesperson to discuss the value of the product with a potential buyer. Will selling the product strongly affect the overall success of his or her company? If so, is it worth the risk of not having it to sell? Is it the kind of product that is in such high demand that it "sells itself"? These factors may remove a buyer's concerns about risk.

3. **Determine how long a guarantee will last**

   The length of a guarantee should be one of the first things discussed when offering one. The longer it is, the longer your company takes responsibility if a product does not sell. Look for balance between one so short it does not inspire confidence and one so long that a potential buyer may take unfair advantage of the promises included.

4. **Discuss the value of what a potential buyer will receive when redeeming the guarantee**

   What will a potential buyer get for your promise? Will it be money, a service, or additional product? Will it be worth more or less than what the buyer initially spent? Spelling this out carefully will be crucial in the contract-writing phase.

5. **What are the terms and conditions of the guarantee?**

   Again, spelling this out carefully will be crucial in the contract-writing phase. Instruct your salesperson to explore every "what if" with a potential buyer to ensure that all parties agree upon any and all terms and conditions put forth.

6. **Use prudence in developing a contract—get it all in writing!**

   Encourage your salesperson to carefully delineate the expectations of both the buyer and seller in the contract, to be clear and precise in his or her language, and to consult other team members or leadership as appropriate. By doing so, the buyer clearly understands the terms negotiated, and the salesperson is absolved of any repercussions that would result from a lack of sales.

7. **Ensure you can deliver on what is promised**

   Do not guarantee sales that cannot be generated. Consider your product—is it one that will continue to be relevant, current, and on-trend in the current market? Will its salability be long-term? Does this product move quickly? Is it one that is highly consumable? Doing initial legwork and having this information available for your team member to discuss with a potential buyer will provide all parties with peace of mind.

8. **Discuss a "best-case" and "worst-case" scenario**

   What is an acceptable goal? What do successes and failures look like? Is there a plan in place to resolve how to correct what may be happening if sales are poor? Have your salesperson discuss a best- and worst-case of an agreement between your company and a potential buyer. Essentially, there are two layers of customers that must both be satisfied with the results.

9. **Provide low-risk options**

   Consider your client—does it have the capability to move the product easily? Can it effectively sell the product in the amount requested? If not, it is wise for your team member to advise the client not to over-order. It is much easier to get more of a product than to have a surplus to unload. Providing lower-risk options, including smaller inventories, similar and less expensive models of a product, or suggesting a sample sale to generate interest is advisable, especially in smaller companies.

10. **Engage risk-reduction tactics**

   Remove the angst involved in having a buyer demand a guarantee by reducing the amount of concern of risk he or she may feel. By agreeing to share the responsibility for any potential loss, your team member can assure the potential client that together you are a unified front on the sales floor, and the product will move. Examples include offering a free trial of the product, providing a buyback option, or offering a discount or bonus upon making a purchase.

If there is one thing your sales team should be able to guarantee to a potential buyer, it is the ability to trust him or her implicitly. A potential buyer should leave a meeting with a member of your sales team feeling confident and well assured that the product will sell and that, if it doesn't, prearranged corrective actions will be taken. Actively listening to concerns, discussing all factors at length, allaying concerns about incurring risk, and providing ways to reduce it should be tactics every salesperson on your team can easily employ to close the sale.

You can't make everyone happy. You're not a jar of Nutella

—Martin and Mayhem

EXCUSE 8

The Buyer Is Overbought
and Not Open to Buy

There is a certain rhythm to sales, and all salespeople must find it for themselves. The relationship between salesperson and buyer is a bit like a dance—timing is everything. If the two are out of sync, sales don't occur. Imagine that, as a business owner or sales manager, one of your team members returns to the office after an appointment. When you ask how it went, he or she says the buyer was overbought and had no open to buy. This scenario can be incredibly stress-inducing for a salesperson, and he or she will often leave a meeting without follow-up. Upon hearing this, you say don't worry and move on to the next buyer. Without knowing it, you have accepted this excuse and inadvertently left the door open for your team to use it again to justify poor sales. Instead of offering a permissive reply, consider the following, perhaps more productive responses or suggestions:

1. **"Okay, try again"**

   Encourage your team member to make a second attempt with the buyer, especially if the buyer is a repeat customer. Suggest that if they cannot commit to a purchase at this time, that the two come up with a timeframe that may work better, so there is still a positive result, even if it is not immediate.

2. **Don't get angry—let cooler heads prevail**

   You may find this excuse (especially if you've heard it before) unacceptable or a sign of laziness, but attempt to stay neutral. If you consider your team member's position, staying calm might be easier to do—he or she is likely frustrated, anxious, and already rather unhappy. Adding your negative feelings to the mix will only exacerbate the situation.

3. **Take a time out and go back to basics**

    Most of us learn best by example. This would be an ideal opportunity for a learning or teaching experience. Take a lesson from your favorite major league baseball team: if all the hitters are paid extremely well to do their jobs, then why do these organizations spend hundreds of thousands of dollars on batting coaches? The truth is, even the best players need to practice staying sharp. Though it may seem tedious, investing time in your team members will pay off in sales. Going back to basics is a great way to reconnect and build confidence to get back in the game.

Now that you've discussed what happened, getting to bottom of the problem is also in order. A few points to consider include the following:

4. **Is your salesperson new to the business?**

    If this is the case, it's likely he or she did not know how to respond to the buyer and let nerves get the better of himself or herself. If it's a more experienced team member, consider other factors, including whether management provided adequate information about the client.

5. **Does this customer have a sales cycle?**

    As I mentioned, there is a rhythm to sales. Many industries have a sales cycle. For example, the retail industry operates from season to season. If a salesperson is calling on buyers out of season, of course he or she will have trouble. Imagine your sales team is attempting to sell winter coats to northern hemisphere department stores in February or bathing suits in August; they are too late. This topic should be reviewed regularly with your team to prevent this mistake.

6. **Review how to respond to a buyer's refusal to buy**

Discussing what to do when a buyer says no before you send your sales team out to meet with one may help them to settle their nerves when they can't make a sale. Remind them that sales is a relationship and that even if they do not make a sale today, their customers will remember how they were treated. For example, without being pushy, a salesperson may ask the customer, "If you didn't have these spending limits, would you be interested in our service (or product)?" If yes, then further conversation can take place, and perhaps an opportunity to make a sale at later scheduled time is possible. If the answer is no, then it may be that a reevaluation of the pitch is in order.

7. **The buyer gave your salesperson an appointment for a reason—their job is to buy**

Most sales meetings are not cold; they are scheduled. Often, the buyer has very limited time and will not offer a meeting time to be polite. Remind your team that being well-prepared, organized, and focused can be the difference between a yes or a yes but later and a no.

8. **Have a plan of attack when you go back**

I like to use baseball metaphors with my sales team. A professional baseball player who is a top hitter only gets a hit one third of the times he goes to bat. Why? Because, more times than not, he either lost his concentration, or his technique got sloppy. Using this logic, I restate the buyer's objection to myself, revisit my presentation, and decide whether I gave a compelling reason to buy my product or service. If I have not, I rework my presentation until I do and try again.

9. **Don't take a no personally—you are your own worst enemy**

Taking a no in sales personally is a confidence killer but is a hard thing to avoid, even for the toughest-skinned salesperson. Over the years, I have given many presentations only to later see that the buyer had picked up a competitor's product. The first thought for many would be *The buyer didn't like me*, but that is not always the truth. It may be that a competitor had a better price or could procure the product more easily, or it could be due to any number of other reasons that had nothing to do with me personally. Doing a bit of research about my competitors beforehand and sharpening my presentation with them in mind served me well and helped close sales.

We hear no every day, especially in sales. How we respond to it can be the determining factor between getting a no every time and getting a future yes. The combination of timing, confidence, and being adaptable will always serve a salesperson better than simply saying, "The customer was overbought and was not open to buy." The most effective management keeps its sales force inspired, engaged, and receptive to change.

Sales is an outcome, not a goal. It is a function of doing numerous things right starting from the moment you target a potential prospect until you finalize the deal.
—*Jill Konrath*

I Am Experiencing
Technological Difficulties

Technology has greatly benefited society at large. It has allowed the modern salesperson to become better informed, more organized, more efficient, and worldlier. What once took hours or days to accomplish can now be done with an exchange of a few emails. Cell phones are pocket-sized computers. Expectations are such that one can and should be accessible and "on" anywhere at any time. We are more accessible, more adaptable, and better equipped than ever to reach our goals and make the sale. This, however, comes at a price. Just because we are ready to work doesn't necessarily mean our devices are. Despite our best efforts, technology is not perfect, and technological difficulties are both common and unavoidable, particularly on the road. They can test the patience of even the most tech-savvy salesperson and bring his or her work to a screeching halt. It is too easy for a salesperson to say, "My computer is down, and I can't get the order," but this is not a reasonable excuse. Here, I have suggestions for how you can coach a salesperson through this scenario and how to encourage his or her ingenuity.

1. **Be well-prepared**

   Regardless of whether technological difficulty becomes an issue during a presentation, a good salesperson is well prepared with a contingency plan. This may include ensuring that a backup computer is available, a paper copy is available, having a presentation committed to memory, or backing up the presentation via a jump drive or cloud storage. The presentation may not be as polished as it would be otherwise, but the contingency plan may very well salvage what could have been a complete failure.

2. **Communicate with your client**

   Technological difficulties happen to everyone and can generally be worked around. Instruct your sales team to tell their potential client what is happening. It is likely that the client has been in the same position and will be empathetic. In fact, he or she may have a solution your sales team member may not have considered. Rescuing the sale is well worth a small amount of discomfort.

3. **Don't panic**

   Remind your salesperson to remain composed, clearheaded, and professional when experiencing a technological issue in front of a client. Also, how a person handles a potentially embarrassing situation may be very revealing to clients and may also influence their final decision. As the famous deodorant commercial jingle says, "Never let them see you sweat."

4. **Use another method**

   Suggest to your sales team member that, if available, he or she use another device. While a tablet or phone may not be ideal, it can help finish what was started or, if nothing else, gather information.

5. **When all else fails, get it on paper**

   A computer is not the only way to store information. Though a technological difficulty may result in a bit of a time suck, there is no reason a salesperson cannot record the needed information with a pen and paper and upload the information to a database later. With some quick thinking and the use of common sense, less time is wasted, and a potential buyer likely will be impressed by your team member's ability to think on his or her feet.

A technological issue is not necessarily the nightmare situation that a salesperson may first picture. In fact, it could very well be an opportunity to display resiliency, self-sufficiency, and grace under fire. It may train your team in tools they didn't know they had or teach them something about themselves. Though every factor of a difficult situation cannot always be controlled, your salespeople can control their own behavior.

Buyer does business with you, not with your company and not with your technology.

—*Mark Hunter*

EXCUSE 10
Our Customer Signed with Our Competitor

Competition is the ultimate threat to a small business. It can be difficult to anticipate how you can be bested by your competitor—be it with lower prices, a better location, better stock, or an overall superior experience. Even the most experienced small business owner or sales manager may not see the threats competitors introduce and can shocked when his or her most loyal customers sign on with another business.

A change in customer loyalty without warning can be devastating. I have had this experience both as a salesperson and as a small business owner, and it has given me valuable perspective. When I first began as business owner, I enjoyed a very successful first year and was looking forward to continuing to build my business during a second, equally successful, year. In my industry, the philosophy was simply "you get one hour once a year to sell for the next year." So, I met with one of my most important customers with whom we did very well during the first year. In my mind, I felt assured that the second year was going to be even better than the first. About two weeks after the meeting, I had not heard from the client, so I reached out to the committee chairman, who told me he had given the contract to a major competitor. I was so shocked and surprised, I almost fell out of my chair! It took a lot for my business to recover: I had to take a road trip from New York to Chicago and then on to Memphis and over to Miami to open new accounts and expand the business. After a lot of effort, the second year ended well. With determination and hard work, during my third year of business I earned back the business I lost from my customer, and I never lost them again. I can say with pride that over the past twenty-five years, I have never lost another client. This experience helped me develop four basic rules for customer retention and customer loyalty:

1. **Do not abandon your customers—you'll miss them when they're gone**

   The end of a sale is not the end of a customer relationship. Like any other relationship, it needs to be nurtured, and your salesperson must maintain an open line of communication. Instruct your salesperson to check in with your customers from time to time to ensure they are happy with their products. Sending holiday greeting cards or quarterly promotional offers to loyal customers helps them keep your company in their thoughts. Your salesperson should remind them that he or she is looking forward to their next contract or meeting. It is a reassuring feeling to valued, and this will help make the salesperson their first choice when seeking out a business partner. This kind of special attention does not go unnoticed, and it is extremely helpful with word-of-mouth advertising. Clients can be your salesperson's best friends in this regard.

2. **Get feedback from your customers, then use it!**

   When a customer provides feedback or suggestions for your business or products (within reason), listen to them! Your customers know what they want; if your company can't provide it, they will likely take their business elsewhere. When your salesperson listens to what they have to say, and your company incorporates their suggestions, it shows customers that you take feedback seriously and want to give them the best possible experience. When they felt heard, they have no reason to seek out your competitors, and you have no reason to fear losing their business.

3. **Discuss new plans with customers—make them part of the team!**

    Your customers want to know that they can count on your business for years to come. To gain their trust in you and your business, your salesperson must show that he or she is ambitious and innovative and that your company knows what it's doing. Including customers in your future business plans allows them to be part of what you have designed and see how integral they are in bringing about these changes.

4. **Never stop improving presentations—show that you're willing to grow!**

    In order to evolve as a business, you and your sales team must be willing to grow. By continuing to polish presentation skills, your salesperson demonstrates to clients that he or she is staying current on trends, your company's products or services are still their best option, and that your company has responded to their feedback or suggestions.

Sales managers and small business owners must continually and consistently remind their sales team that business is all about opportunities, timing, and knowing your competition and your customers. Whether your team takes these opportunities is dependent on their attitude and drive; thus, leadership must set an example. In general, a salesperson directs his or her focus and efforts at one mission: making the sale. There is, however, more to the equation than sales alone. A good salesperson should be expected to seek out customers and meet with them, listen to their complaints, and work to have necessary changes made. A great salesperson also closely monitors the activities of his or her competitors and anticipates a next possible move. The best salesperson is not only proactive but reactive. This not only contributes to the health of the business but allows the sales team to be focused and productive in their work.

As a small business owner or sales manager, maintenance of your customer base should be your number one priority. Treat customers with respect, provide them with the best possible experience, and be open to change. With a solid, loyal client base, you will enjoy years of successful business without worry. Without one, you have no business at all.

And while the law of competition may be sometimes hard for the individual, it is best for the race, because it ensures the survival of the fittest in every department.

—Andrew Carnegie

SECTION II

As a small business owner or sales manager, you will always be coaching to maintain the efficiency and effectiveness of your sales team. This includes continuously updating your sales team with the latest information and incorporating mentorship into your regular team meetings.

The excuses in this section may come from your most successful senior salesperson or your greenest newbie. You just need to coach and continuously coach.

> A coach is someone who tells you what you don't want to hear, who has you see what you don't want to see, so you can be who you always knew you could be.
> —*Tom Landry*

EXCUSE 11

The Economy Is Bad, and Nobody Is Buying Anything

The economy is not reliably stable, and no one person alone can control it. Social and political factors, technology, and the availability of capital and resources all influence its strength or weakness at any given time. This puts you and your sales force in a rather difficult position when the economy is not healthy. When customers cannot make purchases, salespeople cannot make sales. Though this may be incredibly discouraging for a salesperson and an easy excuse for not performing well, it is not the time for despondency. When working as a united front, an industrious management team with its ability to encourage and inspire its salespeople together with a proactive, diligent sales force can overcome even the bleakest economic conditions.

I recommend employing the following sales tactics during an economic downturn:

1. **Focus less on fear**

    Even the most seasoned salesperson may experience fear in times of adversity, but it should not rob him or her of resilience and resolve. It is perfectly natural to feel anxious about future success and the potential for failure, but these thoughts must not be allowed to rule your salesperson's actions or curb his or her enthusiasm. Though it is important to stay aware of economic developments, it is also important to stay motivated and driven. Times like these will test one's mettle, but one may also find oneself inspired to find new ways to meet goals, seek out opportunities for education, and collaborate with fellow salespeople for assistance and support.

2. **Remember that the best defense is a good offense**

Though an economy may be bad, not every person will be equally affected. It would be dangerous to assume that simply because a sale could not be made with one customer the same will be true for all potential customers. Some may still have money to spend or view your product or service as necessity. As the small business owner or sales manager, now is the time to meet with your sales force to develop a plan to accommodate concerns of both repeat and new customers and to discuss how to allay their fears, as well as your own. When a plan is in place, encourage your salesperson to reach out to his or her most loyal customers, reassure them of his or her willingness to explore other options with them, and encourage them to continue their business with your company. This might also be an ideal time to do a bit of networking—word of mouth advertising is some of the best, and perhaps they may be able to connect your salesperson to others needing your company's services.

3. **Get the scoop on your competitors**

On the other hand, the best offense is also a good defense. Do your homework, find out what your competitors are offering, how they price their goods or services, what kind of promotions they use, and how they spread the word (social media, print, etc.). You and your sales team may be able to use this information to modify your current methods, examine what is or is not working for you, and develop a new plan of attack.

4. **Develop an alternative pricing option**

The aim of any business is to maximize profit, but this goal may not be attainable during times of economic uncertainty. You must adjust your expectations and be content with any profits that can be garnered. There are multiple ways the small business owner or sales manager may develop alternative pricing options, including loyalty rewards, new customer discounts, offering free samples, or adding an additional good or service to a preexisting package.

5. **Prioritize your opportunities again**

A bad economy does not benefit anyone in sales. A company that once looked like a profitable new prospect may lose their luster. This is an ideal time to examine leads, potential partners, and prospective clients and evaluate the time and resources that can be dedicated to pursuing them. Perhaps your salesperson has been spending too much time on one client only to receive limited returns or empty promises of a sale; it may be time to move on to another. In these instances, time is literally money, and it should not be squandered.

6. **Double up on your network**

An economic downturn may be the ideal time to reconsider how your salesperson networks. Do current techniques allow your salesperson to reach his or her intended audience in the way they prefer? Are there more efficient, effective ways to do so? Consider the benefit of finding other outlets for networking, including social media, community awareness events, TV and print ads, and word-of-mouth advertising from trusted, loyal customers.

7. **Stay true to you**

If you provide strong management and your salesperson is using successful sales tactics, then encourage him or her stick with them. Though your salesperson might need to exercise some patience in the process, consistency will bring success, even in the direst of economic situations. Additionally, achieving sales goals will provide your salesperson with the self-assurance needed in better economic times to achieve even continued success.

8.   **Find joy in your work**

A downturn in the economy is not a complete disaster, nor should one allow it to make every day a disappointment or a challenge. Even when things look discouraging, it is important to consider the parts of the job that bring satisfaction—is it interacting with new and interesting people? Is it the thrill of the sale? Is it the playfulness of negotiation? Encouraging your sales force to seek out opportunities will help to raise morale, remind them why they do what they do, and hopefully push them to continue to reach their goals, despite a bad economy.

Though a salesperson cannot always control external factors that affect sales, he or she can control attitude. Keeping your sales force united, inspired, and well connected to their client base may not resolve every issue that comes your way during these difficult times, but it will keep you afloat.

Our greatest weakness lies in giving up. The most certain way to succeed is always try just one more time.
—*Thomas Edison*

EXCUSE 12

Our Requirements Are Too Stringent or Too Numerous

Your company may require customers to agree to a litany of requirements. A store may have to be approved by corporate before being allowed to resell your product. Or pictures may need to be taken inside and outside to see if your company wants a product sold in that store. Or your company may want products displayed in a certain way, and the retailer has to buy a fixture to display it.

Here, feedback and excuses from a salesperson about requirements must be carefully evaluated and addressed. Here, listening will serve you best; a customer's comment or objection is crucial to the success of your business and must not be disregarded. When a customer says your company has too many requirements, it is imperative for your salesperson to understand his or her perspective. Ideally, your salesperson should ask two basic questions of the customer lodging these complaints before reporting being unable to make the sale:

A. **Which requirements concern you?**

As always, your salesperson must listen to his or her customer. Is there a clear requirement of concern? If not, your salesperson should ask open-ended questions to help find it and then see what can be done to resolve the issue.

B. **Do many customers share the same concern?**

Look at the concerns of past customers—are there identifiable patterns? Is there repetition? It could be that two customers have discussed your product, and both conclude that your requirements are too stringent or numerous. It could also be that many of your customers have come to the same conclusion independently. Other customers, however, might see things differently and may have their own, very specific, concerns. For the small business owner interested in maintaining a strong, loyal customer base, every concern should be addressed, regardless of what it is or the number of people affected. By actively listening to customer feedback provided to your sales team, you may make appropriate judgments and adjustments as needed.

Upon identifying potential problems and their roots, you can then develop a strategy for resolving them.

If the concern boils down to tools or training the salesperson did not have, ask yourself the following questions:

1. How many of the requirements does the customer have a problem with? This is very important to determine what can be done to resolve the issue.
2. Is it a requirement that is flexible? If so, what alternatives or adjustments can be offered?
3. Can a requirement be completely restructured to suit customers' demands?
4. What are other policies can be added to the existing ones to make things better? Maybe you only need to make minor adjustments to address the problem.

If, however, this feedback has come from multiple customers, additional research and actions will be required, including the following:

1. **Convincing customers that their concerns are incorrect and why**

This may be a difficult feat to accomplish, but if you are firm in your beliefs that your requirements are appropriate, teach your salesperson to demonstrate how and why.

2. **Restricting requirements**

After your own internal review, you may find that adjustments do, in fact, need to be made to the stringency and number of your company's requirements. Take both your own experience and customer feedback into careful consideration and restrict accordingly.

3. **Presenting other plans and visions of the business to the customers**

Have your salesperson invite customers to be part of your improvement process by presenting other plans and visions of your business to them. They will likely appreciate the opportunity, and doing so may solidify a lifelong customer relationship.

4. **Reassuring yourself and your salesperson of the reasons for the requirement**

It is easy to become carried away and to want to make changes based on what customers have said. Your company, however, has developed the requirements for a reason. Though it is wise to consider others' perspectives, do not discount your own. In the end, you know what is best for your business.

5. **Reading about similar businesses and how they run their things**

Learning more about how other businesses in the field operate may be both useful and inspirational. It can help determining what your company should and shouldn't do or be a valuable resource for polishing what may already be solid requirements. Again, trust your own instinct as well.

Every company has requirements; some are flexible, some are not. You should review your requirements with your sales team annually, if not every six months. But before this, you need to review them yourself to see if specific requirements are still applicable or can be modified or deleted. It is surprising to me to see how many inflexible requirements a company has while performing sales audits, which is why I tend to ask for the rationale for a specific requirement. For example, many companies still require customers to complete and sign a formal paper application for each new account. In this day of electronic information storage, there is no reason the process needs to be so cumbersome.

After completing this update, review the requirements with the sales team and explain which requirements are flexible and which are not. Your team especially needs to be prepared to discuss the logical reasons for inflexible requirements to a prospective buyer. In my experience, if you give a logical answer as to why a requirement is inflexible, the buyer usually accepts it.

For flexible requirements, you should provide parameters that the salesperson can use. These parameters can then be employed when applicable; for example, your terms of sale may not be flexible for new customers but may be for a loyal customer or large-scale one. Ensure that every rationale is explained to your sales team.

Managing the stringency and number of requirements is a continuous process—one in which your sales team is actively involved. A regular requirement review process with your salespeople trains them on how to anticipate and overcome objections to close the sale. In addition to performing regular reviews, include updates to inflexible requirements and their logic as well as the flexible requirements and their parameters in the onboarding manual, so all employees can see the process from the onset. In my experience, this, in part, helped prevent this excuse and empowered my staff.

Small business ownership comes with its fair share of difficulties, and one of most difficult is always maintaining customer satisfaction. There will be times when "the customer is always right," and there will be times when customers are not. Fostering open lines of communication, listening to their concerns, and trusting your own instincts will make negotiating expectations around requirements less stressful and more productive for everyone involved.

Obstacles don't have to stop you. If you run into a wall, don't turn around and give up. Figure out how to climb it, go through it, or work around it.

—*Michael Jordan*

Our Sales Literature Is Missing or Incorrect

In general, people tend to best absorb new information visually. Having a visual aid to complement a presentation allows people to digest what they have learned, reminds them of important product details like price, and serves to summarize key points of a presentation. In sales, a visual aid is essential. It is nearly inexcusable for a sales team member to not have written material about the product to leave for a potential buyer, because buyers will almost always ask. One of the most important qualities of a successful salesperson is creativity. Employees who are proactive should be able to develop some sort of literature even if they have none available and be able to correct information if available literature is inaccurate. This can be easily accomplished using software like PowerPoint or Photoshop that are designed for creating media like sales literature.

I've always believed that a good salesperson leaves something behind or sends a follow-up email to a potential client after a presentation. When I first began my career in sales, I developed several different pieces of sales literature to fit the circumstances that I encountered. Most of the time, it was a customized piece that I scribbled on paper and then asked the design team to develop and fine tune. I have often used freelance graphic artists for this purpose as well.

Recently, I assisted Macy's Home Division in launching a high-end product line. We needed to develop training information to educate store personnel in seventeen seminars throughout the United States.

This cost the company a minimum of $30,000 in fees and related travel expenses.

All the literature that was available focused on the product line's features and contained nothing about its benefits. The store associates who were to be trained would be selling to consumers who really want to know what these benefits are, but the company had no literature on this information! This would have left the store associates in a disadvantageous position. It also ran the risk of making it seem as though they did not know their product well, leading buyers to lose confidence in the seller, and hence, a loss of sales.

To address this issue, our team developed a brochure that not only addressed the features but also described the benefits to the consumer. We constructed it from existing literature by reworking it to suit the purpose of the product line, adding information particular to the line, and addressing potential topics of interest or concern to a buyer. Additionally, we hired a freelance graphic artist for $200 to provide design and format styling, and had it printed at a local print shop. We printed 2,500 of these brochures (to train over two thousand sales associates), for a total cost of less than $500.

Effective sales literature should have the following characteristics:

1. Brevity, which keeps the attention of the reader. Too much information may become tedious or overwhelming to a potential buyer. Most of the time, buyers know what they want; what they want to know from your salesperson is whether your company can deliver it.
2. An attractive appearance, with clear, detailed images, a sleek design, and a color palate that is pleasing to the eye. Also make sure they are stored in a place where they will not be torn, stained, or crumpled.
3. Legibility—when designing your literature, take font, color, and space into consideration. Is it easily readable?

4. Pertinent phrasing and images.
5. Current, up-to-date contact information for your sales team member, as well as contact information for your sales manager or business owner. Additionally, if available, provide website and social media information (e.g., Facebook, Pinterest, Instagram, or LinkedIn).
6. The most essential benefits of your product, presented in a succinct but attention-capturing manner.
7. A price and options list (e.g., colors or sizes), if applicable.
8. Clear instructions for what to do with the information they have received. Indicate where the contact information is on the literature, provide a business card, and assure them you are available for questions or concerns at any time.
9. Inspiration for your buyer to act immediately—instructions for how to place an order and with whom. If they are available, coupons, discounts, or other sales promotions may entice a potential buyer further.

The results of our efforts yielded very positive results. The sales team started to do the seminars, and the feedback that they got from associates was tremendous. The associates felt it was simple, to the point, and answered the questions consumers had about the product. Many sales associates asked if they could keep a personal supply of them so they could give them to the consumer when discussing the product.

The associates also asked why the other companies giving seminars did not have literature like this, as it was so beneficial to the consumer. Several associates contacted the sales team weeks after the seminar and told them that the brochures we had given them often helped close sales.

Note that each sales team member will have a different approach to design materials, and if the essentials are addressed, you should encourage creativity and an active interest in preparing these documents. As the adage goes, "a picture says a thousand words." If that's true, imagine what the combination of strong visual aids and a solid sales presentation can accomplish.

I think it's fair to say that personal computers have become the most empowering tool we've ever created. They're tools of communication, they're tools of creativity, and they can be shaped by their user.

—*Bill Gates*

EXCUSE 14
Our Product Line Is Limited

People, by nature, like variety. Most of us enjoy having the most popular, fashionable, or up-to-date version of a product available. It is difficult to sell someone anything less, especially when the customer has a model or type in mind, or their options are limited. It leaves a salesperson in the difficult position of trying to sell what your company offers, with limited success, or explaining to potential buyers why your company does not carry what they are looking for. It also puts your salesperson in the equally difficult position of determining whether he or she agrees that your company's product line is limited, how to demonstrate that it is sufficient (if he or she disagrees), and how to incorporate more options, if necessary. It is a double-edged sword: if you choose to expand your line, you run the risk of losing money by investing in items that don't sell, but if you don't, you run the risk of losing potential clients because of a limited line. This is an ideal time to open a conversation with your sales team to find out where this feedback is coming from and whether it is the opinion of the sales team or the clients. Your team will know your potential buyers best, and their opinions and concerns should be considered if your business is to stay competitive and successful.

Developing a solid product line often involves years of collaboration with designers, marketing teams, factories, and production teams. If you have done your due diligence in building the product assortment, you should be able to justify every product in the line, why it exists, its intended target audience, and how its features and benefits compare with competitors in the same space. This, however, does not mean the product line should be neglected or not kept current. You will need to perform consistent and regular reviews to ensure that what you're offering sells and, if it doesn't, where improvements and updates can be made. Regular review with your sales team is also advisable, as they may be able to help plan, as needed.

There is, however, such a thing as too much choice. Offering too many options can be overwhelming and distracting, and it may lead to buyer's remorse. For a long time, a common theory in marketing was that the more choices a customer has, the better. The logic was that people like options, so providing more flavors should produce more sales. However, in 2000, psychoeconomists and authors Sheena Iyengar of Columbia University and Mark Lepper of Stanford University published a relatively simple study.[3] A table was set up outside an upscale market in Menlo Park, California, laden with a variety of jams. On two consecutive Saturdays, research assistants who were dressed up as store employees offered samples of either six or twenty-four flavors of jams made by Wilkin and Sons, a British jelly purveyor known for exotic flavors.

When twenty-four flavors were offered, 60 percent of people stopped to sample the jams, compared to 40 percent when only six flavors were offered. These numbers seemed to favor more choices, but the question remained: which group purchased more?

Of the customers who sampled twenty-four flavors, only 3 percent purchased jam; of the customers who sampled six, 30 percent made a purchase.

If you modeled this study based on a sample of one hundred people, when twenty-four flavors were offered, sixty shoppers would stop, but fewer than two (1.8) would purchase jam. When six flavors were offered, forty shoppers would stop at the table, and twelve would purchase jam.

As you can see, there is a paradox: contrary to popular belief, providing too many choices can be bad for sales. Customers can be attracted to the idea of having many choices, but when it comes time to make a

---

[3] Iyengar, S. S. and M. R. Lepper. "When choice is demotivating: Can one desire too much of a good thing?" *Journal of Personality and Social Psychology* 79, no. 6 (2000): 995.

purchase, too many options can make decisions difficult and lead to fewer sales.

When I began my career in sales, I worked for GAF selling cameras and film. Kodak was the king, and GAF was second. No other competitors were on the market at that time. We often performed demonstrations at stores, featuring products from our ads. A potential buyer came up to the counter and would make the simple request for a roll of film. I would then ask: "Slide or print?" "Twenty-four or thirty-six exposure?" and "GAF or Kodak?" I now realize I confused customers with too many choices, for their response was "Let me get back to you," which almost always meant a sale was lost.

A senior sales associate who saw this happen came up to me and said, "Keep it simple, and ask them if they want slides or prints, and twelve or twenty-four exposures, then give them a roll of GAF. If they want Kodak, they will ask." This was excellent advice, and I found that by offering some choices—but not so many as to overwhelm—I made more sales and had better success getting my product out.

When it comes to providing a well-crafted product line, simplicity is key. Give your potential buyers enough options that they feel they have a good range of choices, but don't provide so many that they are immobilized by indecision. Provide a few options from every price range, from the most high-end and elite models down to the lower-priced, more economic models. Give your sales team an inventory they can speak to well and confidently; then listen to their feedback when they provide it, and make corrections as needed. In a way, you, your salesperson, and your buyer are a team. When everyone has what's needed to do his or her part, that's when the magic happens.

Everyone has limits. You just have to learn what your own limits are and deal with them accordingly."
—*Nolan Ryan*

We Do Not Have Any New Products

In the chapter about having a limited product line, I discussed how people like variety as well as the most up-to-date version of products. Although presenting a potential client with too many options may be overwhelming, it is also difficult to sell someone limited options. It can truly be a challenge to sell what your company has available, particularly when it is a product line a buyer has already seen.

Many factors may explain why no new product is available, including that the line is already current, that no funds can be allocated to extending a product line, that the products will no longer be sold and are being phased out, or that new products are currently unavailable due to unexpected factors (e.g., issues with importing, product is sold out, or factory issues). Buyers, however, are generally not concerned with these excuses and will take their business elsewhere to get what they want. Sometimes it takes a bit of fancy footwork, some artistic license, and a test of loyalty for a salesperson to close the sale. It may feel discouraging, but it is not entirely impossible. A combination of honesty and optimism, when well placed, can be enough to encourage return customers to continue to patronize or to motivate a new client to do so. Here, I identify scenarios, discuss solutions, and help develop a script for a sales team member in this situation:

1. **The line is already as current as possible**

   Though this may not be what a buyer wants to hear, it may be that no new product exists because it is at its most current. Update product lists and price sheets to reflect production or release dates so your salesperson can show customers that they have the most up-to-date version and provide them with release dates for future models when available. That way, even if a sale cannot be made, it is not necessarily lost but simply postponed.

When a buyer expresses concern over this scenario, a salesperson can say, "I understand that you are looking for new product and that you are disappointed right now. As you can see, the new model of this product will be coming out later this year, and I would love to schedule a time to demonstrate it and get your opinion." Additionally, it may be that a comparable product in the line may be of interest; if so, the salesperson should present that as an option. It should be relatively easy to illustrate how it compares and why it might be even better.

2. **We cannot afford to extend our line at this time**

You should be performing regular reviews to ensure that what is being offered will sell. In an attempt to offer customers a variety of options, it is easy to overextend and overspend. For a new business, time and capital, which may not always be immediately available, are required to build a solid product line. It can be humbling to cite expense as a reason your company does not have more options, and it may give the impression that your business is not thriving or committed to addressing customer needs. Therefore, it should be reframed in a positive way. For example, if a potential buyer asks why there is no new product, a salesperson could say, "We are very selective about the products we carry in order to provide you with the best and most affordable products on the market and feel our current offerings do that. If we do not have what you're looking for here, I would be happy to share comparable products on our line that might also suit your purposes." By being presented a similar option, buyers will still feel like they have freedom of choice.

3. **These products will no longer be sold or are being phased out**

A savvy buyer will always be looking for a discount or a deal—a savvy salesperson will always find a way to provide one. Offering options, such as loyalty discounts for repeat customers, half off, or two-for-one sales, may not only encourage sales but also provide a good salesperson with the opportunity to unload inventory that isn't moving. In addition, providing a potential buyer with a taste of what the future might bring might sweeten the deal: "Though they are of excellent quality, we are in the process of phasing out this line of products. We have priced to it move in order to prepare you for our newest line." This way, buyers are still assured of quality but may also be curious to see what will be coming next, encouraging them to become or remain repeat customers.

4. **A new product is not currently available due to circumstances beyond our control**

Some situations in sales cannot be anticipated and may be difficult to explain to a potential client. For example, a company may just not have money to invest in inventory on a new product. Hopefully, for return clients, brand loyalty is enough to weather these rough patches. But people are impatient, and your salesperson may encounter clients who says they plan to look elsewhere to get what they want immediately. Again, a savvy buyer will always be on the lookout for a discount or deal, so, if possible, combining the use of an honest answer with a bit of incentive for loyalty might be an ideal solution. For example, your salesperson could say, "As much as I would love to get that product out to you right away, there is a current backlog in supply for it. May I offer you a rain check or put the item on backorder at the current price, once it becomes available?" If clients feel valued and respected, there is a high likelihood that your sales team will find success and rescue the sale.

As consumers, we have all experienced times where we felt disappointed when we were unable to get what we wanted when we wanted it. Unless it is an emergent situation, one can usually find incentives to try the next best thing, experience something new, or simply be patient. Keeping this in mind, encourage your salesperson to flip the script on potential clients and to practice the golden rule—sell to clients as you would want to be sold to.

Change your thoughts and you will change the world.
—*Norman Vincent Peale*

EXCUSE 16

We Do Not Have the Inventory

They say variety is the spice of life. This is particularly true in the sales industry. Business is in a constant state of evolution, and if you don't evolve, you lose both income and clientele in short order. A wise, competitive business owner or sales manger knows that to stay on trend and to increase sales, you must employ the skills used by your competitors and seek out innovative ways to surpass them. One effective way to do so is to ensure your inventory is varied, relevant, and in regular rotation to account for poor sales or lack of interest in a model and to ensure your salesperson can offer products that are in high demand.

How Useful Is an Inventory?

Generally, a well-maintained inventory is necessary. It is an asset that allows you to calculate the worth of what you have. Additionally, an organized inventory provides unseen benefits. Among one of the most important is that it can reduce business taxes: in some states, businesses are taxed on the amount of inventory they have at the end of the year. Another benefit is that inventory can be used as collateral for a loan if it is valuable enough. In the consumer products market, it is not unusual for company to use a factory or bank that will lend money based on the inventory in the warehouse.

Maintaining an inventory that is attractive to customers requires attention to detail, knowledge of the market, and a bit of savvy. Below are some suggestions for doing so:

1. **Fine-tune how you predict and forecast—polish your crystal ball**

   Predicting and forecasting the market are two vital processes, and they must be done with precision and accuracy. They require you to stay well informed on both general market matters and those specific to your business, research innovations in your product line, and get inside the minds of your customers. This is no easy feat, but with the right tools, successful predictions depend on the following:

   a. Marketing efforts—You may plan to develop a marketing effort via advertising, internet, and viral social media content. You may end up short on inventory, but there is no way you to predict it.

   b. Predicted growth and the economy—You set out with acquired and internal data to determine sales growth and ensure you have enough inventory to support it, but a number of reasons, such as weather, can impact your actual sales. For example, if you are a winter coat company, in an extra cold winter you may not have enough inventory while in a warm winter you may have too much.

   c. Promotions—if you have historical data on promotions, seasonal situations affecting those promotions may not be relevant now. A spring sale that was a disaster because of weather might be a booming success in summer, which will affect your inventory differently.

   d. Market trends—One vivid example was right after 9/11, when the government decided that no carry-on luggage could be brought on board a plane; it had to be checked. Prior to that, carry-on luggage had been the best-selling size. It caused inventory to be out of balance, with too many carry-ons and not enough mid- and large-size luggage. This created havoc for most luggage companies as the government kept changing policies.

2. **Convince your customer with what you have—make a mountain from a molehill**

It is possible that your company does not have the inventory your customer has requested, or you don't anticipate carrying it in the foreseeable future, if at all. An important rule in business is that every customer counts, and their opinions and preferences matter, even if they seem small. You cannot afford to lose even a "small" customer to your competitors. If you no longer carry the inventory a customer needs, it may put your salesperson in a difficult position, but the best option is to proceed with the inventory you do have available and see whether the customer's needs can be met with another product. If your salesperson knows your inventory well, and it's varied enough, he or she can likely find a solution acceptable to both parties.

3. **Mark low-turn stock—out with the old, in with the new!**

Maintaining low-turn stock benefits no one. It holds down sales, leading to a loss of income and a potential loss of customers, and takes up space that could be better utilized with a more desirable product. This stock should be identified and removed from rotation. I advise developing a timetable for purging low-turn stock. For example, the standard for low-turn stock could be when a product has not been sold at all in six to nine months. Additionally, creative strategies should be employed to get rid of remaining low-turn stock items, including special discounts or promotions, such as buy-one-get-one-free or 50 percent off clearance pricing. Though you may lose some money by reducing the price of these low-turn items, you can reinvest what you made from their sale into new, more appealing stock.

4. **Audit your stock as often as possible—it's as easy as 1-2-3!**

While there are many excellent software programs designed for inventory management, it is good practice to periodically count your inventory by hand. Not only will this help you verify your real-world inventory, it will also confirm that what your software reports and what you have in stock correlate. It will also enable you to be certain of the stocks you have on the ground. There are different techniques you can use to do this, including a year-end counting of every item on hand or quarterly spot-checking of ongoing products. The second option is best for high-demand products or those that are difficult to keep in stock.

5. **Hire a stock controller—leave the counting to someone else!**

An effective sales manager should also be an experienced stock controller and able to know the amount of inventory he or she has on hand during specific times, from raw materials to finished products. Though this may not be problematic for the sales manager of a small business, a large business's sales manager might need to put someone else in charge of stock. This person is known as a stock controller. His or her primary responsibilities are to receive deliveries, process purchase orders, and ensure that received orders align with the inventories on the ground. This will optimize workflow and reduce what could be a serious distraction for a sales manager.

As a whole, these tips can be reduced to three basic ideas—know your market, know your stock, and know your customer.

I attribute my success to this. I never gave or took any excuse.

—*Florence Nightingale*

Our Prices Are Not Competitive

One of the biggest determining factors, if not *the* determining factor, for whether a product will sell is its price. Pricing is a delicate balancing act for a sales manager or small business owner. If the price is too low, you make no profit; if you price it too high, no one will buy. Your inventory must be priced in a way that demonstrates its value. When an item is not priced competitively, it puts your sales team in the unfortunate position of trying to sell it anyway, which can often be a fool's errand. This is, by far, the most common excuse as to why a sale wasn't closed, and is, without a doubt, the fastest way for a buyer or purchasing agent to end a conversation.

Unfortunately, there is no silver bullet to solve this problem, and a compromise must be reached. As is often repeated, timing is everything, and a salesperson usually has only one opportunity to make a good impression. If your prices are not competitive, or you're not willing to adjust them, your salesperson will lose sales almost instantly. On one hand, it requires serious consideration and some ingenuity on the part of your salesperson to get a prospective client to focus on factors other than price. For example, the quality of the product, the service your sales team provides, and your company's reputation may help to convince the client to buy your product. On the other hand, as a sales manager or small business owner, you must ensure that your stock is priced reasonably to prevent these discussions from having to happen.

The following are some suggestions for how to address this issue, both before and after your sales team member has met with a potential buyer:

1. **Do your homework—know your competition**

   To borrow a sports metaphor again, your best offense is a good defense. Ask yourself the honest truth—is our buyer right? Are we not price competitive? No company always has corner on price and profit. Everyone must make a profit and must spend money to develop or manufacture a product. I often ask my sales team, "Do you think our competitors put their pants on differently than us?" The answer is no—we all do it the same way.

   If you are actively invested in your business, you will know your primary competition, the goods or services they supply, how they are priced, and what kind of quality they provide, both in the product itself and in the services of their sales team. Not unlike the coach of a professional sports team, you must accumulate as much information as possible about your competition and give it to the team each week or before each game. It should be an ongoing mission to find out as much as you can about your competitors and to verify what you have learned as much and as often as possible. This does not have to be formal, nor does it have to wait until a sales meeting. It should be done weekly, at a minimum. You should also save what you discover so you can build a book on your competitors. Knowing a competitor's sales team, management or ownership, product line, and pricing gives your salesperson a competitive edge and an opportunity to discover a competitor's strengths and weaknesses and to adjust his or her pitch before meeting with a prospective client.

2. **Make your buyer an offer they can't refuse**

   Often, when buyer say the price of a product is too high, they are simply looking to negotiate a better one. Part of the "dance" of business is negotiation—in a way it can be a bit of fun to find the price point that both parties can agree to, but it can also require a bit of finesse.

If, for example, a permanent price adjustment is simply out of the question, perhaps developing incentives may be helpful. Options could include a first-time buyer discount, coupons, promotion deals (e.g., buy-one-get-one-free or buy-one-get-half-off), or buyer loyalty rewards. By doing so, your salesperson can demonstrate to his or her buyer that your company is willing to meet them at least part of the way to a more agreeable price without having to take too large of a loss in profit.

3. **When all else fails, adjust your prices**

There are many reasons why buyers may say they cannot afford your prices. It could be that they would have to price your product in a way that their own clients would no longer purchase. It could be that they plan to carry more than one variety of the product you sell, do not want to commit entirely to your products, or have a limited budget to spend. It could be that your prices are simply too high for any potential client, and you must lower them. Though it may mean a potential loss of income, it is important to consider that you're already losing income by not making sales at all.

The decision to lower your prices can be difficult, but sometimes it is inevitable. This is a challenging process because you must consider what is best for the health of your business while at the same time attempting to please your potential client base. Consider the prices of your competitors—can you comfortably price your product lower than they can? Consider your bottom line—can you continue to carry an adequate inventory if you lower prices? Consider your other inventory and staffing—are there other places fat can be trimmed to help recover what may be lost? Lowering prices, however, does not have to be a negative action or an admission of failure. It could, in fact, present an ideal opportunity to reexamine how you do business. Perhaps it's time to examine your inventory—what sells and what does not. Perhaps it's time to revitalize your business plan. With the right attitude, it may end up as a positive experience!

It would be a lie to say, "pricing is everything," but words, promises, and loyalty can do only so much to convince a client to buy. At the end of the day, both a sales team and their clients are looking to make or save money—that is, after all, the nature of business. It doesn't mean, however, that we cannot do our best to reach a workable solution agreeable to both parties.

Perhaps the reason price is all your customers care about is because you have not given them anything else to care about.

—Seth Godin

I Do Not Have Enough Leads

Many factors can contribute to this excuse, some of which can be easily dismissed with effective training, coaching, and organization or a willingness to try something new. You have many tools at your disposal to help guide your team, most of which do not require a great deal of resources or time. Below are some strategies for how to get your sales force reenergized, reengaged, and ready to start generating more leads.

1. **Polish your customer service game**

   Sometimes, a return to the basics is necessary. Arrange an in-service for your sales team, and remind them of the importance of exemplary, consistent customer service. Reinforcing the concepts of writing thank you notes, earning trust, being genuine, actively listening, and asking questions to learn more about a client may feel like a waste of time to certain members of your team. It is crucial, however, to instill how important good customer service is in every member of your team—from the greenest new salesperson to the most seasoned veteran. There is merit for everyone in this effort: For those less experienced, it helps develop a core values system. For those with more experience, it helps reconnect them to their work and allows them an opportunity to examine in a critical way how they approach their clients.

2. **Collaborate with your marketing team**

   A marketing team is often an underused resource. They are usually on the cutting edge of consumer trends and know the most effective methods to attract potential clientele. A good sales manager or small business owner should be maximizing the talents of both teams by bringing them together to discuss how to showcase products, how to convince buyers to buy them, and how to combine efforts to create a unified message from the company. When transparency exists and open lines of communication are effectively used, leads should increase.

3. **Get organized**

In sales, it is easy to sink into a rut. You should be regularly considering the nature of your client base and not relying on the same methods for getting new leads each year. The sales landscape is always changing, and you cannot rely on any single approach. Invite your sales team to reevaluate who they are reaching out to and why. Are they still good potential leads? Are they still the intended audience? If not, it may be time to cull your lead list and remove dead weight. This, in combination with learning about new potential clients and observing market trends, can reinvigorate the pursuit of new leads.

4. **Don't ignore the "small" sales**

Every potential client brings value to a negotiation. Some salespeople may consider a client "too small" to reach out to. This, however, would be a mistake. Sales is still an industry that lives and dies by word-of-mouth advertising. A positive or negative experience travels fast in a community. Your sales team should treat every potential buyer like the CEO of a Fortune 500 company. One small, positive experience often leads to more and larger leads.

5. **Follow up on old noes**

A well-organized salesperson should keep a running list of leads, how to reach out to them, and how they respond. Many factors are involved in saying yes or no to a sales pitch, and they are in constant flux. Urge your sales team to follow up on old noes on a regular basis. The first no they receive from a potential buyer will not necessarily mean no forever.

6. **Set goals for developing leads**

One of the most important things you can do as a small business owner or sales manager is to hold your salespeople accountable for creating new leads. If a salesperson is struggling with identifying potential customers, perhaps intervention is necessary. This could be through coaching, goal setting, or providing additional counseling if goals are not met. Ideally, this should not feel like a disciplinary action but rather individualized attention that will help that team member rise to the occasion.

7. **Reduce low-yield lead generating efforts**

When a salesperson is reevaluating how leads are generated, he or she should also consider whether those methods are effective. For the most part, it is well understood that cold calling is coming to an end; potential clients value a more personalized, connected experience. Suggest to your team that they cut back on large numbers of unfocused cold calls and double down on researching a potential client before they make contact. Much can be learned from a quick Google or social media search. This will help a salesperson tailor a presentation or determine whether his or her product is even appropriate for the potential client, saving hours on the phone or emailing.

8. **Make technology work for you**

In the same breath, it is important to note that simply searching for potential clients on the internet without direction is as much of a time suck as making hundreds of phone calls. Your sales teams should be using the technology available to them to their full advantage, including setting up search-engine alerts to notify them when news about a potential client is available, following blogs, and utilizing online meeting platforms to conduct presentations instead of spending time and money on unnecessary travel. By targeting specific industries, selecting potential clients carefully, and narrowing outreach efforts from very general to very specific, your sales teams' productivity will increase, and more appropriate leads will be generated.

9. **Develop and cultivate a social media presence**

   With the death of the cold call comes a precipitous growth in the importance social media. This is an ideal space to develop leads. But your social media profiles are only useful if they are active. Potential clients will use these platforms to research your company, view your products, read reviews, and provide feedback that future clients can see—all of which could make a significant difference in the number of leads generated. Your sales team should be regularly interacting with potential clients, following up on comments and questions, and using the opportunity to speak with them to generate sales.

10. **Tag team**

    As the adage goes, "Many hands make light work." A collaborative effort between members of your team will result in a larger number of leads. Taking a divide and conquer approach, where each salesperson is given a task at which they excel (e.g., assigning cold calls to someone who is skilled at making them versus a tech-savvy pro to work social media) will keep everyone engaged and feeling successful, and it will make everyone's job a bit easier.

A sales team member in a slump can become unstoppable with a can-do attitude, an esprit de corps, and adequate support from management and leadership. Sometimes, it takes being led to lead!

Everyone needs a coach. It doesn't matter whether you're a basketball player, a tennis player, a gymnast or a bridge player.

—*Bill Gates*

EXCUSE 19

The Purchase Order
Has Been Delayed

As a business manager or small business owner, it is extremely important that you delineate the difference between a purchase order (PO) and an invoice for your newer sales team members. Though the two are similar, they have different meanings for a salesperson. Whereas a buyer drafts a purchase order, a seller drafts an invoice. Both can include the terms of sale, but only the purchase order protects a salesperson if, for some reason, a buyer refuses to pay. A purchase order is binding contract, and once it is submitted, reviewed, and approved by both parties, a seller is obligated to deliver and the buyer is obligated to pay. It is essential for a salesperson to ensure he or she receives a purchase order from every customer, with no exception. Not only is it the only way to hold both parties accountable, but it ensures that the received goods are correct in number, type, and price and are delivered on time. It may feel like an annoying, unnecessary formality, but having this paper trail gives both parties a starting place when dealing with any problems that arise. Delays in the submission of a purchase order add unnecessary time expenditures to and cause frustration in the sale process. I recommend the following suggestions for how to resolve potential delays and get the sale back on track:

1. **Check in with your buyer to ensure they wish to continue**

   A delay in getting a purchase order may be a sign of cold feet. Perhaps a buyer is wary of entering into a binding contract without additional thought, budget review, or verification of want or need for your product. Encourage your sales team member to check in with buyers to verify whether they plan to submit a purchase order and, if possible, to set a date for when this might take place.

2. **Offer to amend the purchase order to assure buyers are getting what they want**

If a potential buyer is having second thoughts about making a purchase, instruct your salesperson to amend the details of a purchase order until the buyer is satisfied.

It is easy to agree to a plan when both parties are present, enthusiasm is high, and both want to please the other. But if left alone after a presentation, buyers may use the opportunity to raise concerns, particularly regarding their budget. Suggest your salesperson attempt to be helpful—but not so helpful as to undercut the sale.

3. **Remind the buyer that a purchase order is a valuable tool**

Instruct your salesperson to remind a buyer that a purchase order confirms that the order was correct when comparing it to the shipping paperwork and the invoice. It is also useful for bookkeeping, particularly for tracking how much is spent, how often, and how many units of a product are ordered.

4. **Ensure your buyer is familiar with how to submit a purchase order**

An important question to ask your salesperson is whether the buyer knows how to submit a purchase order. Not every company uses them, so this may be a foreign experience for a client. If the buyer is hesitant to submit one, your sales team member should discuss their benefits and share some examples of past purchase orders to reassure the buyer that they are not as intimidating as they sound.

5. **Walk the buyer through the process**

A buyer may need a little nudge to submit a purchase order. By being persistent and checking in, a salesperson can help him or her stay accountable. Offering to walk the buyer through the process step by step may also allow the salesperson to ensure that a PO is completed correctly. This is a small investment of time that could save hours of phone calls and messages.

6. **Offer to simplify the process**

Obtaining a PO should not be a difficult feat, and there are many simple paper-based and electronic options available that even a first-time user can navigate. Encourage a potential buyer to go paperless—not only does it ease bookkeeping, but it also provides an easier way to track where POs are going, who received them, and the status of an order.

7. **Ask to speak with the person who approves a purchase order**

The path to obtaining a PO can be littered with obstacles, including those outside a buyer's control, particularly in terms of the PO's approval. It may be helpful for a salesperson to ask a buyer for the name of the person responsible for approving POs and to follow up directly with that contact. Have the salesperson note the buyer's name, describe what was agreed upon, and offer any assistance or information that can be provided to move the approval along.

8. **When in doubt, refuse to proceed until a PO is submitted**

There are times where a potential buyer may be prolonging the process for reasons that are not entirely honest, including an inability to pay upon demand, waiting until the last minute to make a payment, or stringing a salesperson along while fishing for a discount or an extra perk. Advise your salesperson to embrace his or her inner skeptic when suspicious this is the reason for a delay, and instruct him or her to refuse to move further in the sale process until an approved PO is submitted. Without it, the salesperson does not have the assurance that the buyer will honor the prearranged terms.

Purchase order delays can be a waiting game. This does not mean, however, that actions can't be taken that will help move the process forward. Your sales team should use tact and resourcefulness, and they should "trust their gut" when negotiating the terms of a purchase order; they should also be a resource to a potential buyer.

Circumstances may cause interruptions and delays, but never lose sight of your goal.

—*Mario Andretti*

EXCUSE 20

A Customer's Technical
Question Requires Research

As consumers, we all want assurances that the products we choose will be user-friendly, work the way we want them to, and be easy to manage should an issue arise. For big-ticket items, many people take time to consider the pros and cons, do extensive product comparisons, and experience dissonance over spending large amounts of money. In sales, a choosy buyer can lead to a discouraged seller. Buyers will likely have many questions, including ones a salesperson is unable to answer, which means this salesperson must consult other resources inside the company. A buyer might also expect an answer immediately, and he or she may be impatient for a reply. This expectation can be particularly aggravating, because this type of buyer will often take a long time in deciding. The longer the buyer contemplates, the longer it will take to make a final decision, and they may even talk themselves out of the purchase altogether. This leaves a salesperson in the difficult position of determining how and when to do a full-court press, how much attention may be too much, and how to salvage a sale when it appears to have stalled out. Here's how you might approach this situation:

1. **Clarify the question being asked**

   Sometimes a person asks a question but is not entirely sure about what they want to ask. To prevent potential confusion and further delay, instruct your salesperson to repeat the question back to the client, verify that he or she understands the client's concern, and ask clarifying questions if needed to direct a course of action.

2. **Try to do some basic footwork**

   Suggest to your sales team that showing a good-faith effort to find an answer is very telling of their willingness to go the extra mile. Persuade them to find an answer for the buyer on their own as soon as possible and remind them what this small gesture can do to build a positive customer service experience.

3. **Assure the buyer an answer will be provided shortly**

   Though this may not always be entirely true, encourage your salesperson to check in regularly with a potential buyer regarding their question. Ideally, this will help to reassure the client that your salesperson has passed on the question to a member of your team and anticipates an answer shortly. This indicates that your salesperson is dedicated to finding an answer and is doing his or her best to get one.

4. **Thank buyers for their patience**

   Often, a frustrated customer is simply looking to be heard. When your salesperson checks in with buyers, instruct your salesperson to thank them for their continued patience and ask how your company might improve their experience. If there is an easy fix, the salesperson should offer it.

5. **Reward clients for their patience**

   When most people reflect upon a time when they were annoyed by having to wait, it was often made less annoying by being rewarded for their patience. For example, when dining out, if the food is particularly late, the waitstaff or management may offer a discount or free appetizer to placate an angry customer. If a potential buyer is threatening to take his or her business elsewhere, offer a small discount as thanks for waiting. As the saying goes, "You can catch more flies with honey than with vinegar."

6. **Call in reinforcements**

If a salesperson cannot answer a technical question, it may be easier to allow him or her to discuss it with another staff member. If a buyer has a question about how a product can be modified, it may be easier to connect the buyer with a production manager to save time, cut out the middleman, and provide the opportunity for follow-up questions. Additionally, connecting buyers with someone like a sales manager may help make them feel important and heard, which could help to persuade them to continue to be patient.

7. **"Keep calm and carry on"**

Remind your sales team that a potential client may be unpleasant to deal with because they are unhappy with waiting and not with them or their product, and, if they are feeling stressed, to allow themselves a moment or two to regroup and reassess the situation. Remind them to remain positive and friendly and to look for any opportunity to improve the customer service experience in order to keep the sale afloat.

8. **Show follow-through**

If a deal is struck, make good on it! If a potential client is expecting a return phone call, follow up with your team to make sure this was done. Recording these details somewhere is the best way to ensure all expectations are addressed and met.

9. **Keep your own customer service experiences in mind**

Invite your sales team to remember scenarios where they were in the buyer's position. What convinced them to wait for an answer? How were they treated? Did they feel they got the answer they wanted? Suggest they keep these thoughts in mind when tailoring their approach to a buyer's question.

10. **Close the loop**

> Finally, when the question has been answered, make sure your sales team closes the loop. Was it the answer the client wanted? Does the client have additional questions? Have any action items resulted from the conversation?

Ideally, a salesperson can answer every question during his or her presentation. However, this is rarely the case. Preparation, consistency, and remaining dedicated to providing an exceptional customer service experience will serve your team well in closing even the most difficult sales.

> Products and services can easily be replicated. So, if your company's competitive advantage is based on products and services alone, you are at risk. But if it's based upon products, services, and quality service, then you'll have a competitive advantage that's very difficult to match.
> —*Lee Cockerell*

SECTION III

The excuses in this section may seem unbelievable, but as a sales manager and small business owner I have encountered them all. If you encounter these excuses for not getting orders, you should seriously think about the capabilities of your sales team or organization and whether the person offering these excuses is a right fit for your business.

When it's time for me to walk away from something, I walk away from it. My mind, my body, my conscience tell me that enough is enough.

—*Jerry West*

I Do Not Have the Correct Price List

I consider a salesperson not having an accurate, up-to-date price list to be truly careless. An up-to-date, correct price list is an essential tool in the salesperson's toolbox. Without it, a salesperson is like a chef without a set of knives, poorly prepared to make a presentation. It also demonstrates to both the potential buyer and the sales manager or small business owner that this employee is not dedicated to his or her role as a salesperson.

The onus of developing a correct price list, however, lies with you, the sales manager or small business owner. It is completely irresponsible for you to send your sales force into the field with inaccurate information. Doing so will take a toll on the effectiveness of your team, and, in the end, the business will suffer for it.

To a certain degree, responsibility for maintaining an accurate price list should be shared—salespeople should know their stock and an estimated price for each item, and they should check in regularly with management to ensure no changes have taken place. Management should have one centralized price list, designate the person responsible for updating it, distribute updated information regularly, and check in with the sales force to ensure they are using the correct list.

As a small business owner, I realize this sounds much easier than it is. I learned the hard way, as, at one point, I had several different price lists for the same products at the same time. This was incredibly frustrating for both me and my team. The first thing I had to do was review the process for developing a price list and designate someone to be responsible for publishing it, whether it was the marketing manager, the production manager, the sales manager, or myself. The process of making a price list will generally result in several revisions. In this digital age, it can be very easy to distribute an old version. If you have designated someone other than yourself to distribute and maintain this list, you must clearly delineate the process with them, as well as your expectations for how and when it will be done.

You or your manager is responsible for the sales team. This person ensures the team sets goals and focuses on them, checks their data, motivates team members, and organizes training programs. Additionally, he or she engages with customers, addresses their complaints, analyses the budget, knows how to streamline them, and stimulates more sales. This implies that this person is responsible for everything involving sales, including the price list.

When a salesperson is not adequately equipped with an accurate, up-to-date sales list, you must take swift and immediate action to prevent further errors or complications that may result in a loss of sales. These include the following:

1. **Interview the salesperson—do a little detective work**

   This is a serious issue and must be regarded as such. Ask your salesperson about his or her role to ensure he or she fully understands the basics of the position. The salesperson may need to be reminded of these basics to reengage with his or her work. Review pertinent data and records with him or her to get to the root of the problem.

2. **Build confidence in the salesperson—pump them up!**

   Your salesperson may be experiencing a lack of confidence or some insecurity about his or her performance, making it difficult to effectively carry out assignments. Such distractions can lead to carelessness, including using inaccurate price lists. Showing your support and understanding for where your salesperson is and how he or she feels may give your salesperson the confidence that he or she is not alone and can feel comfortable speaking with you when are challenged. This should improve your salesperson's overall productivity.

3. **Provide relief in duty for the salesperson—help him or her refocus**

   If your team member shows no remorse for his or her mistake and no willingness to improve, it is advisable to remove that person from his or her duties and substitute a more competent salesperson. The fact is, danger looms when a salesperson is not functioning as he or she ought to, even more than when working with a brand-new employee. Sales are affected, as is profit. It may be necessary to reassign this team member to nonsales duties to provide time and space to refocus his or her efforts on the basic responsibilities of a salesperson. Giving your salesperson a final opportunity to reflect upon whether to remain a member of your team, time to recharge, and a chance to regain your trust will be invaluable and help determine the course of his or her career with you.

4. **Replace the salesperson—sack them!**

   The time may come when it is apparent that you have exhausted your ability to retrain, recharge, and reengage your sales team member, and you must make the difficult decision to end your working relationship. Though this is an unfortunate and often uncomfortable experience for both parties, if your salesperson refuses to come to work prepared, it is inevitable.

5. **Prepare a soft copy containing the price list—give the new guy a "cheat sheet" to help them learn!**

   When onboarding a new sales team member, it may be easier if you can make the price list available in a soft copy such that the team member can easily consult it when he or she seems confused or requires clarification.

Your success in sales, at the end of the week, is the result of your sales force's competence and how effectively you and your sales manager have carried out your roles. To set reasonable sales goals, reach them, and push yourselves beyond where you thought possible, you must work together as a cohesive, communicative, unified unit. When everyone is on the same page, especially the page containing the price list, your team can be unstoppable.

Laziness is nothing more than the habit of resting before you get tired.

—Jules Renard

I Get Distracted by My Phone and Lose Focus

As a sales manager or small business owner, you will face every kind of excuse—like the ones in this book—as to why a sale was not made or why a quota was not met. In these cases, your employee may not want to attribute the failure to his or her own inadequacies or incompetence. Despite your best efforts to coach and encourage your team, your salesperson may not have realized the importance of a presentation and how distractions like taking calls, texting, or browsing the internet on a phone can make one appear unprepared, unprofessional, and unlikely to make the sale.

I have spent my adult life selling or managing sales. The excuse discussed in this chapter has been around since cell phones proliferated twenty years ago. Before drawing any conclusions, however, it is important to ask yourself, —does the salesperson understand how a presentation works and what is it we are trying to accomplish when we make one?

1.   **What is a presentation? Is it really that important?**

    Your sales force should understand that a presentation is essentially a performance where a salesperson exhibits or demonstrates the product being sold. The salesperson not only showcases the sample, but also provides every necessary detail needed to persuade a customer to purchase the product. The onus is, therefore, on the salesperson to create a welcoming, memorable, and informational presentation. Most of the factors that determine a presentation's success are carried out before and during the presentation. Your sales force must be keenly aware of these factors and take into consideration the things that will help close the sale.

2. **Concentration—get your game face on!**

Professional athletes and Broadway performers prepare themselves mentally before performances, getting themselves "into the zone." They may spend time alone to avoid potential distractions. Like them, a salesperson needs to be similarly disciplined and focused to make a professional presentation.

I have personally experienced a distracting situation, so it is easy for me to empathize. On that occasion I arrived at my client's office just as I received a thought-provoking, though not life-or-death, phone call. I became distracted and lost my concentration, and when I entered the client's office I was disorganized in setting up my display, showcasing the samples, and making my presentation. It was not my finest work, and I was extremely disappointed in myself. I was, however, able to reschedule the presentation for another time and achieved a much better result.

After that presentation, I developed a cardinal rule: I turn my phone off at least two hours before a presentation so as not to be interrupted by a text or phone call. To maintain open lines of communication and to prevent unnecessary concern if I do not immediately reply, I inform others that my phone will be turned off two hours before every presentation.

3. **Giving a professional presentation—are you a pro? Act like one!**

In general, your sales force will not be 100 percent efficient with their presentations. There is always room for improvement, and that comes from effective training. The professional athlete and the Broadway performer spend many hours practicing in order to perform at the highest levels, and your sales force should be no different. One way to do this is to make sure that coaching resources for effective presentations are available to your team. These resources include books, videos, recorded lectures, and shadowing opportunities with colleagues. Simulated practice presentations within your organization may also be beneficial. For example, you could allow each salesperson to present while you and other team members provide questions, potential conflicts, and feedback as a potential customer would. After the practice session, discuss successes and challenges and explore as a group how best to refine the presentation further. This would be an ideal place to address any potential distractions, identify pitfalls presenters experience when distracted, and suggest ways to prevent them.

4. **Know your employees and their strengths—knowledge is power!**

    A good sales manager knows his or her team like the back of his or her hand and is acutely aware of each team member's strengths and weaknesses. This knowledge should help you delegate tasks to team members based on their respective abilities. For example, a salesperson who is not adept at multitasking and is easily distracted should not be assigned presentations while overseeing customer concerns at the same time. If you need to fill a secondary role or position, however, perhaps he or she may be better suited to take that on. Knowing your how to optimize your team members not only sets them up for success but also prevents errors, delays, and poor customer service experiences.

5. **Observe—your eyes don't lie**

    As previously mentioned, a client presentation should be taken seriously. It is a serious job and must be treated as such. Sometimes, however, having a bit of reassurance from a colleague can get your salesperson through a difficult presentation. If a junior salesperson continues to feel distracted, unfocused, or easily intimidated, you may suggest he or she have a senior salesperson observe a presentation. This person can, if necessary, step in and assist the colleague if a challenge presents itself. Ideally, the junior salesperson will pay attention to how the challenge is resolved, and, over time, will be able to manage similar problems on his or her own.

Even the most seasoned salespeople will find themselves lost at sea on occasion during a presentation, usually at an inopportune moment. Remind your team that allowing themselves a quiet moment to mentally prepare beforehand, avoiding potential distractions, getting additional training, and asking for help when they need it will help them focus and get back to shore.

The secret of concentration is the secret of self-discovery. You reach inside yourself to discover your personal resources, and what it takes to match them to the challenge.

—*Arnold Palmer*

My Presentation Was Rushed

There is a certain degree of truth to the saying "Time is money." When time is at a premium, customers look for the most information in the shortest window. This can leave a salesperson who prefers face-to-face appointments at a disadvantage. The buyer no doubt has other appointments, meetings, and tasks to attend to, most of which may have a higher priority than a sales meeting. As a result, the salesperson may feel pressure to rush through a well-prepared presentation while trying to keep the buyer's attention and preventing the buyer from feeling his or her time has been wasted. A rushed presentation can leave even the most levelheaded and composed salesperson rattled and unsure, which can result in the lack of a sale.

A rushed presentation benefits neither party. For example, if misunderstandings about expectations or deliverables are not addressed during the presentation, they may continue to be neglected when a contract is negotiated. If a presentation is rushed, the customer may not have enough time to ask questions, and the salesperson may clearly define the terms and conditions in a way that the buyer fully understands. As a result, both parties may enter an agreement uninformed and later discover that they did not, in fact, agree on the same terms. As a result, feelings of mistrust may develop on both sides—the buyer feeling manipulated and the salesperson feeling as though there was a breach of contract. This, in turn, may lead to the loss of a repeat customer at best and potential legal action at worst.

To easily eliminate misunderstandings before they reach this level, the buyer and salesperson should take proactive measures to prepare themselves for the meeting, including scheduling time for discussion and allow questions. A few helpful tips include the following:

1. **Prepare preemptively (but not too much)**

    Though your salesperson may find it tempting to send a hard copy of the entire presentation to a potential buyer prior to meeting, instruct him or her to resist the urge. It may seem like a time-efficient maneuver, but it could minimize the perceived need for face time with the salesperson. I have noticed that whenever one of my salespeople mailed a proposal to a potential buyer before a meeting, the buyer felt like it was fine review it at his or her leisure. Your salesperson might assume buyers will probably not do so, but they could and as a result might decide before he or she even makes a proposal. Additionally, if buyers have already decided, it is likely to increase the chance of them rushing your salesperson through his or her proposal or canceling the meeting outright.

    Note: I think the best time to send a proposal is after the meeting (despite leaving one with the buyer), with a cover letter recapping the meeting and addressing answers to the buyer's questions.

2. **Ensure your salesperson speaks directly with the buyer**

    An assistant can be helpful for filling in for small amounts of time (e.g., when a buyer is running late to a meeting). An assistant should not, however, be the stand-in representative for the entire meeting. An assistant will often say he or she can brief the buyer in the salesperson's absence, but this rarely happens, and, if it does, the assistant might miss vital information. Additionally, this person may not be qualified to ask necessary questions or understand a process, which could be damaging to a sales pitch.

3. **If the buyer is unavailable, postpone the appointment to a more convenient time**

    If the buyer has a time constraint, he or she may be willing to reschedule to a more convenient time. This will put both parties in a more advantageous situation to better discuss and negotiate.

A well-prepared salesperson has rehearsed a presentation and will know how much time it takes and how much time to devote to questions and discussion afterward. If, for example, a salesperson knows the presentation will require one hour but the buyer only has thirty minutes, he or she should suggest postponing to another time where they will have a full hour. By being clear about expectations, a salesperson can remain in control of the topic and time, which ensures that both parties will be engaged and attentive.

Note: When your salesperson asks to reschedule, it is best to inform the buyer that it is to ensure have adequate time for the presentation. It is not wise to for your salesperson to suggest that he or she has another meeting booked, for example, or is concerned that the buyer will make him or her feel rushed.

A well-run, healthy business with aspirations of longevity is one where there is good rapport between customers and the sales force and where there is mutual respect of each other's time and effort. Both parties should feel that their time is valuable, that what they have to say is important, and that the other party is actively listening and wants to hear what is being said. It is a genuine disservice to both parties to simply go through the motions of participating in a rushed presentation, as there is not only the physical expense of travel, salaries, and materials, but also the much more valuable expense of time. If either side feels disengaged or disinterested, a sale is unlikely, meaning that your salesperson's efforts were wasted.

Customers don't care at all whether you close the deal or not. They care about improving their business. It is way to forget this in the heat of a sales cycle.

—*Aaron Ross*

We Are Not a Big Enough Company to Handle Them

When your salesperson comes to you with this excuse, it is indicative of your salesperson's lack of confidence in the company. You cannot allow this excuse go unanswered, as it may even spread to other employees. Even though the statement could be very much correct, it does not change the fact that the sales team should always be positive. This excuse certainly must not be repeated to customers, as it could affect further transactions with them.

Usually when I hire a person or am confronted with this excuse, I relate one of my previous experiences. In the early days of my company, one of the three big automobile companies approached me after seeing one of my products in a large retailer and liking it. They wanted me to make a component for one of their automobiles. I went to several meetings and also met with their design team; this was a big project for two years. The amount of work, coordination, and effort was way beyond what had I anticipated; however, the contract was significant—it was going to more than double my sales at that time. I was asked if my company was big enough to handle the project. Without hesitation, I said yes and proved to them that I had the necessary equipment, resources, and talent to do it. I believe my straightforward responses to their questions about manufacturing, quality control, and materials satisfied their concerns. I won the contract, and up to this day, I do not understand why they didn't look further into my company's background to see if we were really capable of pulling off the project, as we were quite small then.

In addition to meeting this excuse with a previous experience, I would give the salesperson suggestions on how to respond when a prospective customer believes the company is too small. For example, I would develop an "Objection Document," which I would amend and update from time to time. This document should list the top twenty-five objections that potential customers in your industry could bring up and then list one to three bullet point responses for each. The responses from my "Objection Document" would include the following:

1. Our company can give high-quality attention because we have industry experts with over XX years of experience. You will be in constant contact with them. I have come from a larger company in the same industry; I would not be here unless I knew we could handle your business
2. Unlike most larger companies, we are much more agile and can adjust to your needs easily and quickly. We do not have a variety of different departments that require approval for changes
3. Is there a specific concern you have that I may be able to answer or get someone from my company to meet with you about?

If you want to execute a project for a bigger company, your sales force must let them know your terms and the price. It is wrong and a sign of weakness to try to offer them a lower rate or other incentives to win the project for yourself.

Lastly, your company might need to step up your game to make a deal happen with a bigger company. These step-ups can include increasing your capital, raising more money, good proposals, and others. It is crucial that your salesperson presents himself or herself well, and it vital to present the firm well, too. Even if your company does have not enough capital, showing intelligence and a clear understanding of the customer's size concerns during the presentation goes a long way in the long run.

America was not built on fear. America was built on courage, on imagination and an unbeatable determination to do the job at hand.
—*Harry S. Truman*

I Am in a Slump

As a sales manager or small business owner, you now that not all news from your sales force will be good news. The world of sales is often unpredictable, and a drop in productivity can be truly frustrating to your team. You may hear words of disappointment, pessimism, or discouragement so strong that you may think your salesperson wants to quit sales entirely. Slumps are normal and relatable. Even professional athletes at the top of their game can experience a slump from time to time and have difficulty getting back in the game. A good sales manager can recognize when a staff member is in a slump; a great sales manager knows how to help get that salesperson back up to speed.

A slump can be difficult to identify immediately. It can begin as a gradual decline, building momentum before finally ending in burnout or collapse. In sales, correcting a slump may depend on factors outside your control, such as the state of the economy. For example, in a bad economic climate like a recession, careful and deliberate steps are taken to prevent great losses, and there is little room for error. In a good economy, however, there is less risk involved, and more attention can be given to solving a team member's slump, with better outcomes for all. Despite the best efforts of management, the salesperson must bear the bulk of the responsibility to get back up to speed. The following are steps that can be taken to encourage, educate, and stimulate your staff:

1. **Understand potential causes—what happened and why?**

   This initial step will test everyone's comfort levels but is a necessary one. As a manager, you must approach the situation with caution, compassion, and respect for the staff member, as the reason for this slump may be something personal that he or she is not willing or ready to share. Asking thoughtful questions and waiting for a response before speaking again will open the lines of communication. Are there external stressors? Is there a health issue? Is he or she experiencing symptoms of burnout or a lack of satisfaction? Does he or she feel adequately compensated? If none of these seem to be the case, you should start looking at the fundamentals. You (now a sales coach) will need to review the basic mechanics of selling both on your own and with your salesperson. At some point, all salespeople need a return to basics to remind them of what they do and why they do it. A salesperson may be required to work on the road; he or she will be expected to move from one customer to the next, making sales happen at every turn. If he or she is not meeting quotas, it may be that he or she is not reaching out to enough people. If enough people are contacted but quotas are still not met, perhaps this team member is not persuasive or experienced enough. A salesperson must be cordial, persuasive, and able to communicate well. The solution may be as simple as a back-to-basics refresher on effective sales techniques.

2. **Allow your salesperson to learn from colleagues:—it takes one to know one**

Do a ride-along with the salesperson for a day or two to observe how he or she makes sales, identifying successes and challenges. With this information, you may be able to provide more concrete, reality-based feedback and develop a personalized plan of action to help. Arranging for one of your top salespeople to do a ride along with this colleague may also be beneficial. If the senior salesperson has additional feedback or suggestions for improvement, it should be presented directly to you to prevent the salesperson from feeling scrutinized. Review your findings and the findings of your top salesperson and look for learning opportunities to pass along. For example, does the top salesperson have more experience in particular areas? What are the differences between their approaches? When these learning opportunities are identified, communicate them to your salesperson and encourage him or her to ask questions and seek out support as needed.

Another solution may be to match the salesperson in a slump with a high performer in a nearby territory. The slumping salesperson could use this opportunity to observe the other's technique and develop his or her own sales strategies. After a retraining period, this person should be able to return to his or her own territory and responsibilities. Though this may temporarily result in an empty territory that is not generating sales, the time spent building skills and helping your team member get back up to speed will result in long-term benefits and profit.

3. **Set targets and goals and promise bonuses—put the carrot on the stick**

Targets and goals are positive pressures that are essential in business. They are an incentive for a salesperson to work harder and generally result in stronger sales. Sometimes, to stimulate sales and keep your team motivated, you may promise a bonus to anyone who meets a specific sales goal over certain period. For example, you could set a target where everyone must make at least two hundred sales a month, and an extra award is available for those who sell beyond the benchmark. At the end of the quarter, you may acknowledge a top performer with some form of prestigious award like "the salesperson of the quarter." Those with a strong work ethic or a competitive nature will set their sights upon goals like these, and it is highly likely you will gain additional productivity.

Rescuing a sales team member from a slump can be labor-intensive. Investing your time and energy into his or her development, however, is a strong indicator of a quality manager, shows a good-faith effort to be of service, and demonstrates to the rest of your team that you believe in all of them.

A good coach can change a game. A great coach can change a life.

—*John Wooden*

My Business Cards Are Not Here

As a small business owner or sales manager, sometimes you feel like you are part leader, part coach, and part parent. There are excuses you may think that you'd never hear, or worse, ones where you ask yourself, *Is this person serious?* Perhaps one of the most important tools in a successful salesperson's toolbox is common sense. Unfortunately, like many of our parents said, it can't always be taught. When a salesperson uses an excuse like "My business cards aren't here," you may find yourself wondering why you hired this person in the first place. But this should have no bearing on a sale if your salesperson is good at the job. It also demonstrates an inability to think for oneself and a lack of resourcefulness, and it should raise serious concern about whether this person is meant to be a salesperson. Though it may be tempting to express frustration and anger at your team member, instead, take a deep breath and use this opportunity as a teachable moment. The following are some tips for how to best address this situation, should it arise:

1. **Encourage forethought**

   Remind your sales team member that part of the job is always to be prepared. This includes addressing logistical issues like ordering business cards before running out. You may suggest putting an autorepeating reminder to do so on his or her personal calendar (e.g., monthly) or instruct your administrative staff to have a standing order for all team members.

2. **Utilize social media**

   Social media platforms provide new opportunities to contact a potential buyer. Suggest that your sales team cultivate a professional social media presence if they do not already have one. Include commonly used platforms like LinkedIn, Twitter, and Reddit. Profiles should include contact information regularly printed on a business card; that way, if they do not have a business card available, they can encourage a potential buyer to seek them out online.

3. **Follow up with a phone call**

Because your sales team member should be following up with a phone call as part of his or her sales process anyway, that phone call is another way to provide information to a potential buyer. Additionally, it serves an opportunity to address any questions or concerns the buyer may have and ideally will end in a sale.

4. **Leave a paper trail**

A well-prepared salesperson, in addition to having business cards available, should also have some sort of pamphlet, price sheet, or brochure to give to a potential buyer during a presentation. This document would ideally contain your salesperson's contact information and may be used as contact information in a pinch.

This may feel like a somewhat laughable exercise, but in the end it will benefit your sales team if this excuse ever arises. Ideally, this is a mistake only a very new salesperson would make and an excuse you hear only once. It should in fact not be tolerated more than once; if the excuse is repeated, disciplinary action should follow. For a first offense, however, some redirection will hopefully pay off in a successful sale.

By failing to prepare, you are preparing to fail.
—*Benjamin Franklin*

I Cannot Get an Appointment

Every sales manager or small business owner has done time as a salesperson and knows the challenges of getting face time with a potential buyer. Securing an appointment is perhaps one of the most difficult parts of the sales process. Communication could break down at any point between making initial contact, scheduling a presentation, and making the presentation, whether because of unforeseen circumstances or a lack of buyer interest. A salesperson must quickly learn how to maintain the balance between being persistent and being a nuisance, when to be aggressive versus a bit coy, and how to get what your company wants without sacrificing too much in return. It can be a complex juggling act, but if your sales team is proactive and clever, this excuse will hopefully never come up. But should it, I suggest the following tips:

1. **Do your due diligence**

   One cannot rely on a cold call alone anymore. There are a multitude of ways to reach a potential buyer, and your team should maximize use of all them. Encourage them to Google the buyer, review their social media accounts, and look for useful information, including email addresses, "snail" mail addresses, business hours, and contact information for support staff (e.g., the buyer's administrative assistant or office manager). Learn more about who your team will be talking to and hints for how you might connect to them on a personal level once contact is made.

2. **It's all in who you know**

   It may be that your salesperson cannot reach the buyer but has access to his or her administrative team. All is not lost—these people will know the schedule of the person with whom your salesperson wishes to speak, how they prefer to be contacted, and how willing they will be to speak with a member of your team.

Additionally, it may be helpful to consider who potential clients might have in common. For example, if your organization has a loyal customer who suggested you contact a fellow potential customer, it may help to mention that shared contact ("I spoke with John Brown last week, and he mentioned you were looking to purchase a product like this ..."). This may be helpful in establishing trust, allowing a reputation to speak for itself, and open a conversation wider than what might be accomplished with a cold call.

3. **Read the room**

When making initial contact, there is only one opportunity to set a positive, friendly tone. Again, the onus is on the salesperson to strike a balance between sounding effusive or false, overly formal, overly casual, or robotic. Sometimes, this happens only seconds after a greeting. Encourage your sales member to be confident and to listen for verbal cues that indicate interest, boredom, or irritation. Ensure that they keep these contacts brief and recognize when a no means no rather than an appropriate opportunity to push a bit further to generate interest.

4. **Don't forget the art of conversation**

This is an art that shows the mark of a great salesperson. Almost every potential client wants to feel like a valued individual and can tell the difference between someone who is genuinely interested versus someone who is just trying to make a sale. Encourage your team to be as natural as possible, to ensure they have names and preferred titles correct, and to listen carefully for how a potential buyer responds to what is being said to them.

5. **Be prepared to make a "mini" presentation**

If a potential client expresses interest in a product, a salesperson should be prepared to provide additional information and answer questions. The basics, including prices, varieties, and availability should be memorized or readily available. A potential buyer will not want to wait for this information, and the faster a member of your team can provide it, the higher the likelihood of a sale.

6. **Don't take no for an answer immediately**

Everyone can have an off day, a monetary budget, a time budget, or a lack of interest in a product. That may mean that a no today will not be a no tomorrow. Encourage your team members to note "no" clients and add them to a follow-up list. Perhaps later they will be more interested, more receptive, or have additional resources to make a purchase. Encourage your sales team to reconsider their approach upon a second or third contact to keep things fresh and engaging. Again, the salesperson should be looking for cues as to whether it would be appropriate to contact this potential client again.

7. **Provide multiple options for ways to connect**

Fortunately, not all meetings have to take place face-to-face anymore. Ideally, a sales team member will be able to arrange a face-to-face meeting with a potential buyer by being flexible and providing multiple options, including after-hours, early morning, or weekends, as appropriate. If none of these times are agreeable, they could suggest using a web-based video platform (e.g., Skype, Zoom, Go-to-Meeting). This way, both parties may still put a face to a name, products can be demonstrated, and screens and emails can be shared in real time.

Half the battle of being a good salesperson is being "good at people." Being a good listener is equally as important is being a good talker.

Knowing your product, knowing your audience, and knowing how to bring them together takes skill, confidence, and patience. Though some of this is inherent, much can be learned though solid mentorship and a well-executed plan. Incorporating this training early on with new salespeople may help break the ice and warm up the sales flow.

You got to know when to hold'em, you got to know when to fold'em, know when to walk away.

—*Kenny Rogers*

My Client and I Are Unable to Connect

The excuse of being unable to connect via phone or email is weak, especially given the ubiquity of cell phones and computers. Though it may be both frustrating and challenging to attempt to coach a sales team member who uses this excuse, with some patience and a willing ear you can at least attempt to understand his or her perspective. It may also present an excellent opportunity to provide guidance.

There are few industries today where email isn't the preferred mode of communication. We find ourselves in a time where communication and working styles differ greatly between older and younger generations, which presents obstacles that must be examined carefully and sensitively. Many members of the up and coming workforce (e.g., millennials) prefer using email over making calls; some even say they actively dislike talking on the phone. For their older colleagues, the opposite is often true. Email can be more efficient and more productive, provide a paper trail of conversations, and for some removes the angst that comes with speaking on the phone.

I, for one, agree that email makes me more productive overall, but I also receive at least 150 emails every day. It is difficult to process so many, and it takes great effort to provide a timely answer to them all. Without prioritizing (which often requires additional time), emails may be missed or go without a response for long periods of time. This breaks down communication and delays completing tasks and transactions. It is these times when a phone conversation is either more time efficient or necessary for clarification, making it the preferred means of contact. A thirty-second phone call could be all that is required to resolve an issue.

It need not be a fearsome thing; in fact, it should be an important tool in any salesperson's toolbox, valued as equally as email.

In one of my own experiences, my group had an appointment with a buyer, made a very professional sales call, and were given some follow-up to do. We accomplished what was requested and sent an email to the buyer seventy-two hours after the meeting. We received no response for several days despite our email efforts to follow up. We lost valuable time, a delay that could have been prevented if one of us had just decided to place a phone call.

After a sales presentation, the most appropriate approach is for your salesperson to send an email that recaps the meeting and responds to any unanswered questions, followed up by a phone call. This dual approach provides not only a personal touch, but also gives the salesperson a chance to ensure the email was received and the sent information was reviewed. It also provides the buyer with an opportunity to ask questions, get clarification, or better yet, place an order. For a potential buyer, it is very easy to respond quickly and negatively to an email without giving a salesperson the opportunity to defend his or her position. Remind your sales force to take preventative measures to not allow this to happen. Ask your salesperson to consider the preference of his or her potential client—the buyer may prefer to have a conversation rather than answer another round of emails. Without this second step of a follow-up phone call, the sale will be lost if an immediate response was required.

Though a salesperson may feel frustrated when unable to reach a potential client on the phone immediately, it is possible that administrative support will answer for the client. A connection is still made to a live contact, and he or she may have immediate access to the person with whom the salesperson wishes to speak. If nothing else, the admin team will be able to provide your sales team with essential information, including business hours, a good time to call back, and how this person prefers to be contacted. If your sales team is working with a return client, suggest that they clarify with the office that they are attempting to contact the buyer to resolve an issue or answer a question, so the administrative support staff not assume it is a cold call.

The excuse of not being able to contact a client is not acceptable and may require you to give some "tough love." When coaching your team, encourage them to be persistent, look for multiple methods to contact a potential buyer, use those methods, and follow up more than once with each method. It may also be advisable to develop a company-wide policy for all salespeople that both an email and phone call be used to communicate with a client, which may be met with resistance. Growth is occasionally uncomfortable, but it is when we are learning that we are growing. Allowing your sales team to become too comfortable may make them complacent, from which no party benefits. By making a two-method contact a company standard, no group in your workforce is favored—all will have to force themselves out of their usual process, which may render positive results for them and for the company overall.

Diligent follow up and follow through will set you apart from the crowd and communicate excellence.

—*John C Maxwell*

The Customer Is Not Compelled to Make a Change

When a salesperson makes the excuse that a customer is not compelled to make a change, it gives me pause. This is a major indicator that this salesperson's abilities have not developed. Every good salesperson knows that a customer always retains the right to decide whether to buy the product you offer. If you cannot determine why a customer does not buy from you, it is difficult to present convincing reasons why he or she should. An attentive salesperson knows exactly why a potential customer is not interested in the product, and if he or she is not willing or able to obtain this information from the customer, it is likely his or her career in sales will be short-lived.

In the role of manager or business owner, I ensure my entire sales force understands the common objections customers have for not buying a product, including quality, price, packaging, postsales service, and product awareness. Preemptively incorporating these factors into a client presentation, whether it's for a new buyer or a repeat customer, can not only assure quality but may also convince undecided buyers to patronize your business. Below are some of these objectives and potential solutions to them:

1. **Demonstration of product quality: show, don't tell**

    Quality is a crucial determinant for product selection and is defined as a state or measure of excellence and being free from defects, deficiencies, or significant variations. This is attained by observing a strict commitment to uniform standards that satisfy specific customer requirements. Providing a quality product is beneficial both to the customer and the organization selling it, particularly for repeat customers. A customer loyal to one product will only change to another if the quality of the new product is better than others like it. Your salespeople should know the quality of their product and how it compares to competitors' products. This information should be presented in a clear manner that is easy for a layperson to understand. Ideally, your product is of higher quality than that your customer currently uses, and you can demonstrate how.

Customers like being able to see how a product works. If yours can be tested (assuming you already have the product test results), provide a third-party test result along with that of the customer's current brand. Seeing the two products in action may be a deciding factor to help your salesperson close the sale.

2. **Give your product a competitive price**

   Though quality is an important factor in whether a customer will purchase your product, a sale often comes down to price. When a management team decides upon a price for a product, several things must be taken into consideration, including the cost of production, supply and demand, the costs incurred from importing and exporting, and market competition. The sales manager and his or her team should be an integral part of pricing decisions and must stay vigilant for changes in market trends and the rates of their competitors.

   It is best to price a product competitively but conservatively. Overpricing a product will result in customer loss, and once customers are lost, it is difficult to win them back. Underpricing is equally problematic because it may result in a loss of income until greater sales volumes are generated and because is difficult to raise a price later without also losing customers. One way to resolve this issue, however, is to provide discounts, bonuses, promos, and loyalty program membership to encourage patronage and repeat customers.

3. **Branding and packaging: sometimes it's what's outside that counts**

    When you think about what attracts you to a product as a consumer, what do you see? Good packaging is one of many ways to increase your sales. Sleek design, a well-selected color scheme, and an intriguing logo are all branding techniques that can make a product more memorable to a consumer. The higher the quality of branding and packaging, the more confidence your customers will have in your product. An easy first step to increasing sales during a lull is to rebrand. This may include changing the size of the packaging or the wraps on the products or adding variety to a preexisting product that normally performs well (e.g., adding a new flavor or type).

4. **Offering postsales service: make them miss you when you're gone**

    A little high quality after-sales service goes a long way in businesses. Today, it is more important than ever. For example, imagine someone who sells televisions. A good salesperson can schedule a home visit to the customer to oversee the installation. Though the initial transaction is over, the installation is a postsale courtesy service that will earn the both salesperson and the company a higher degree of trust. Providing exceptional postsale service not only makes the experience memorable for a customers but also increases the likelihood that they will return, knowing they will be treated well. Conversely, poor or unmemorable service will almost guarantee that your customers will take their future business elsewhere.

    Receiving letters, emails, and positive online reviews can be very validating for a salesperson and indicative of a high-quality postsale service experience. Customers may look to these affirmations to determine whether they should patronize your business. Keep in mind that even negative reviews have value because they provide opportunities to make necessary changes.

5. **Social selling: see you on Instagram or Facebook**

   Social media have been a game-changer for sales. As Shannon Belew said in her book *The Art of Social Selling*, "the sales and marketing process has been forever changed; if you do not adapt, then your social-savvy competitors will leave you (and your sales quota) in the dust."

   A proactive, forward-thinking salesperson will develop a strong social media presence, focusing on sites and apps where customers or prospective customers are likely to visit. Even small companies can have a basic presence, using free sites such as Facebook or Instagram as a jumping-off point to build a name for themselves. Here, you can advertise new products with photos, share positive customer feedback, and easily provide information about new products and services. Friends on social media share information about services and products they like thousands of times a day, and this may be your ideal introduction to digital society.

6. **Get customer input on what they want: they're always right, right?**

   A good salesperson should always consider customers' needs and try to anticipate what they want. Paying attention to product reviews and sales trends and listening to customer feedback will help a salesperson learn what a customer values and whether to stay the course or make changes. This attentiveness will encourage product and customer loyalty as your salesperson consistently provides clients with the quality products and customer service that they have come to expect.

Though all these techniques will be valuable tools in your salesperson's kit, common sense should also ring true. When attempting to compel a customer to make a change, your salesperson should reflect upon his or her own experiences as a consumer. What were the deciding factors, either for making a change or against making one? If your salesperson can apply those techniques or factors to a sales pitch, he or she should try it. After all, we are all customers from time to time.

Life is 10% what happens to me and 90% of how I react to it.

—*Charles Swindoll*

I Do Not Have Enough Time

In sales, there is no truer saying than "Time is money." The way salespeople budget their time can speak volumes about their ability, their strengths and limitations, and their work ethic. Unfortunately, time management does not come easily to everyone. Worse still, everyone has a different interpretation of what effective time management looks like. This presents an interesting challenge for even the most seasoned business manager or small business owner, as you must learn, understand, and evaluate how each member of your sales team manages his or her time. When not having enough time is presented as a reason for not making a sale, the management team may feel frustrated—if everyone is given the same expectations and deadlines, why are this salesperson's not being met? The answer is never simple, and you must consider several factors. You must become a detective and ask your team member and yourself some hard questions.

1. **Are my expectations for this salesperson unreasonable?**

    Consider the assignments you've given. Consider the deadlines you've provided. Is the salesperson being asked to cover too many clients at one time? Can he or she complete what you expect in the desired timeframe? Checking in with this salesperson about his or her workload may provide clues about where he or she is spending time and how. Seek out opportunities to adjust as appropriate, whether that includes providing additional time or creating a lighter workload.

2. **Can the salesperson describe his or her process?**

Have the salesperson "walk" through his or her daily schedule. How much time is spent preparing presentations? How much time is spent traveling? How much time does he or she spend face to face with a client? Look for inconsistencies and places where time may be wasted and then discuss whether there are more efficient ways to accomplish these tasks.

3. **How experienced is this salesperson?**

A learning curve may be one reason for large time expenditures. Newer salespeople will be juggling the tasks of learning their role in the company, exploring their territory, researching their potential clients, and beginning to make the initial connections with them. Any one of these tasks will require less time for a seasoned salesperson. If the salesperson is new, give him or her enough time and space to complete these tasks before looking at other factors. Encourage efficiency without sacrificing thoroughness. If possible, share collective wisdom the sales team may have about the territory or clients. If the salesperson is experienced, consider whether there have been changes to his or her role (e.g., added territories or contacts) and whether he or she needs additional assistance to accomplish these tasks while adjusting to the new responsibilities.

4. **Am I providing adequate support to my team?**

Consider the support available to your sales team. Do they have the tools they need to complete their tasks? Is there a clear procedure plan in place? Do they have enough time for travel if they have remote territories? If you believe that the sales team is adequately supported, discuss what may be missing. If no procedure plan is in place, I advise collaborating with the sales team to develop one.

Once the time-suck culprit has been identified, the onus is on you to determine where corrective action can be taken, decide what measures should be employed, and discuss these and the expected outcomes with your salesperson. Once effectively communicated, these should be actionable items with measurable results. They might include the following:

1. **Adjusting expectations**

    If the salesperson is concerned about his or her workload versus meeting deadline expectations, listen to what is being said. If it sounds rational, provide the team member with what he or she feels is lacking, whether that means lightening the salesperson's client roster or providing deadline extensions when requested. Encourage your employee to come to you when feeling overwhelmed instead of waiting until it becomes troublesome.

2. **Provide coaching around scheduling**

    If a salesperson is struggling with time management, provide solid, real-world examples. Perhaps he or she can be assigned a peer mentor to learn a more efficient process. Perhaps shadowing your salesperson throughout a "typical" day may be helpful to provide coaching. A time management book, course, or seminar may also be helpful. Though results aren't always immediately apparent, time management is something that can be learned when one puts in the effort.

3. **Check-ins and wrap sheets**

    The modern office often uses check-ins and reporting tools to keep employers and employees communicating and accountable. Planning regular weekly or biweekly check-ins is a consistent way to provide feedback and resolve concerns in a timely manner. This is an ideal venue to discuss things that may be creating time management problems and how to best resolve them.

Week-end wrap sheets are another valuable tool for time management, particularly for new hires. Here, the sales team member records the tasks completed each week, remaining action items, progress notes, and anticipated deadlines. It serves a dual purpose as a checklist and a way to hold a team member accountable for time-sensitive items. It also demonstrates to you what has or has not been accomplished and why. It can clarify workflow and time usage with easily understood documentation.

4. **Have policies and procedures in place**

The more you can do to prevent a salesperson from "reinventing the wheel," the better. Planning and preparation take time. Having a streamlined, transparent workflow not only saves time but also ensures that all members of the sales team clearly understand exactly what is expected of them so they can incorporate it into their working style. This will open the lines of communication and provide management with usable feedback to optimize processes already in place.

If time is money, investing it into developing your sales force is money well spent. Giving them space to learn, an opportunity to discuss challenges, and tools with which to communicate will serve them best. Keeping your ear to the ground, being open to feedback, and showing a willingness to collaborate to resolve problems will unify your team. In time, the actual money will roll in, too.

It's not enough to be busy, so are the ants. The question is, what are we busy about?

—*Henry David Thoreau*

EXCUSE 31

I Emailed the Proposal

The path from getting a lead to making a sale is never a straight line. There are false starts, detours at every turn, and delays, and sometimes it ends before it begins. Though these obstacles cannot always be anticipated, there is much a salesperson can do to attempt to correct his or course. Of which, the most important is taking initiative and being willing to approach every proposal with equal engagement and effort. People become distracted by outside circumstances, a heavy workload, or feelings of burnout, and dedication can flag. This is when excuses like "I emailed the proposal" usually present themselves. In the name of time management or because of a lack of interest or engagement, a salesperson may try to cut corners by performing the most minimal gesture to attempt to get a sale. But this can go wrong many ways, including a technological difficulty where a client never receives the proposal (e.g., because it is caught in a firewall or buried among other email), a client not feeling it necessary to respond if he or she is not interested, or a client taking offense at not being personally contacted.

Emailing a proposal, unless a face-to-face presentation has already been conducted, should be avoided at all costs. It is not only insincere and impersonal, but one cannot cultivate a relationship with the buyer easily, and buyers do not have an opportunity to see a demonstration or ask questions in person. It may give a potential buyer a feeling of disrespect as well. Additionally, it leaves room for error if a salesperson sends an incorrect file or one that cannot be opened because it is damaged or corrupted. If this occurs, there is then nothing for a potential buyer to review and likely demonstrates to him or her that a salesperson either has no attention to detail, is badly organized, or is simply not dedicated to providing exceptional customer service. Either way, the buyer will probably choose not to work with a given salesperson if this is a demonstration of his or her work efforts, as it may present as sloppy or careless.

This can leave you in a potentially difficult place when it comes to redirecting your salesperson. For one, you must get to the root of the matter to determine why he or she emailed rather than presented the material, whether they the circumstances will be repeated, and how he or she will address the issue. Unfortunately, you may not get the answer you seek. In this case, here are some additional steps you can take to resolve the issue:

1. **Check in with your sales team member**

   Much like a salesperson in a slump, unseen circumstances may be affecting performance. Check in with your employee, offer support, and encourage communication with you when he or she is feeling overwhelmed, stressed, or otherwise distracted.

2. **Encourage your salesperson to follow up with a phone call**

   Instruct your salesperson to call the potential buyer to whom he or she emailed the proposal. This will provide your salesperson with an opportunity to ensure the document was received, address any questions, set up an in-person interview, or take an order.

3. **Monitor your salesperson's efforts**

   Though it is tiresome to both you and your salesperson, a period of monitoring may be appropriate to determine how this salesperson is spending his or her time, whether it is effective, and how to address discrepancies. If you see recurring patterns around making proposals, perhaps this will provide you with enough data to either do some coaching or take disciplinary action. Continue to check in regularly until the issue is resolved.

This excuse generally doesn't hold up and will require you to break what could become a potentially nasty habit on the part of a salesperson. By approaching the excuse with due diligence to get to heart of the issue, you are setting an example for your sales team member, which will hopefully remind him or her to stay engaged, be communicative, and rededicate himself or herself to working as an active, productive member of your sales team.

Success isn't the result of spontaneous combustion.
—*Arnold Glascow*

EXCUSE 32

My Samples or Proposal Did Not Arrive on Time

Before examining this excuse and how to respond to it, it may be helpful to define some terms.

A business proposal is a solicited or unsolicited submission by one party to supply to or buy certain goods or services from another. It differs from an offer because an offer is a commitment whereas a proposal is not. If the other party accepts the proposal, however, the one making the proposal is expected to follow through and negotiate a binding contract. A request for proposal (RFP) differs from other proposals because an RFP is only available in response to a request for a proposal. Most of the time, it constitutes a bid. A proposal, unlike a sample, in most cases comes as a written document presented to the other party.

A sample allows a buyer to determine how reliable and dependable a product will be and to test its quality. A quality sample, as I have mentioned in other chapters, may speak volumes more than any presentation, while a quality presentation reinforces the experience.

In business, one can never account for the element of chaos. Unforeseen and uncontrollable problems that are potentially harmful to operations are bound to happen from time to time, and every seasoned salesperson has weathered at least one "close call" or complete disaster.

I once traveled to Richmond, Virginia, where I was expected to make a presentation for a large account. The day before the presentation, I received a phone call informing me that the sample I was expecting from Asia had just arrived in my office. I instructed my office to send it to the FedEx office for customer pick-up so I would have the samples in hand the next day at 8 a.m. in time for my 10 a.m. meeting. The next morning, much to my anger, the samples had not arrived at the FedEx office, and they were unable to locate the package. When I attempted to follow up with the staff from my home office, they explained that the shipping department sent it to the FedEx office via UPS. The sample never showed up.

Although situations like this can be unavoidable, you can take preventative measures to make them less likely. For example, better planning can prevent samples or proposals arriving late. In the example above, I could have been clearer in my communication with my support staff to ensure the samples were sent in the correct way to the correct location. Perhaps I could have had a contingency plan, in case the samples or proposal did not arrive, such as similar samples, previous models, or document drafts, so the customer had at least some sort of visual aid or idea of the intended proposal.

If a sample or proposal does not arrive to the appropriate destination on time, not only does it send a message that the salesperson is poorly prepared, but he or she also loses an opportunity to use these valuable tools to persuade a customer to purchase the product.

Factors responsible for delayed proposals or samples and their respective solutions include the following:

1. **Transportation delays**

    In general, situations like that of my example are out of the ordinary. One cannot account for travel delays like inclement weather, cancelled flights, or mail delivery issues, but a good salesperson must develop a standing contingency plan to address them so there are no surprises without a clear solution. The salesperson should find out how long specific transportation should take beforehand, keeping in mind both expense and time parameters. I learned from my own late samples and made it a policy to have written instructions for what will be shipped, when it is to be shipped, and when it is to arrive. Since then, I have also made it a priority to obtain and share shipping documentation so that it can be tracked and to avoid further delivery errors.

2. **Technological issues**

   Technological issues are the bane of any salesperson's existence, especially when sending proposals. Network issues, firewalls, program compatibility, and a lack of technical knowledge can all lead to proposal delays. In this scenario, it is advisable to verify the information of the recipient, double check both address and name, ensure that support staff receive a courtesy copy as a failsafe (as available), and ensure that there is a way to verify receipt of the document, with either a confirmatory email or phone call. Additionally, it may be helpful to ensure all users of the document have equal access by verifying that all parties have the correct software and can open the document. Finally, ensuring all parties understand how to use the document's software will prevent frustration, misunderstandings, or general inability to access the work. Employing a user-friendly interface will save time and reduce the risk of delays as well.

3. **Poor planning**

   Of all the potential sources of delay or problem, poor planning is the most easily avoided and creates the highest amount of stress for everyone involved. If I've said it once, I've probably said it thousands of times: PPP = PPR (piss-poor planning equals piss-poor results). This should be a lesson a good salesperson needs only to learn once. He or she is ultimately responsible for the success or failure of a presentation, and poor planning and organization will almost always guarantee failure. By using effective time and resource management, providing clear and detailed instructions, and avoiding last-minute preparations, a salesperson not only relieves himself or herself of unnecessary stress and effort but also reduces the risk of mistakes. One of my other favorite mottoes is "Inspect what you expect." With a solid plan, your salesperson's task list should be completed in advance with enough time to double check his or her work.

Chaos, whether self-induced or caused by outside forces, can leave a salesperson feeling defeated before a meeting with a client even starts. Recognizing that no one is perfect and that we are all prone to mistakes is challenging when you strive to be the best. If your salesperson can learn from his or her mistakes and make every effort to avoid repeating them, he or she will improve as a salesperson and be of greater benefit to your team.

> If you want to make good use of your time, you've got to know what's most important and then give it all you've got.
>
> —*Lee Iacocca*

I Was Busy, and I Missed My Appointment

The life of a salesperson is incredibly busy. Salespeople are in constant motion—traveling, attending meetings, and preparing presentations in addition to maintaining their personal lives. It can all be a bit of a juggling act, and from time to time a ball will get dropped. As a sales manager or small business owner, you must be prepared to receive an onslaught of excuses for why this happened, as well as be able to respond to the consequences. Imagine learning that a member of your sales team missed a scheduled appointment and that when you reached out to ask what happened, he or she replied, "I had to answer emails and forgot." How would that make you feel? On one hand, it could be completely understandable. On the other, this is not acceptable professional behavior.

You need to respond to this situation with both seriousness and urgency. You should ask questions about how this salesperson feels about his or her workload and responsibilities, how he or she multitasks, and how he or she prioritizes tasks. In addition, a formal apology should be issued to the client.

To address the issue head-on, take the following steps:

1. **Ask questions about feelings around workload and responsibility—check in on the checked out**

   Accidents happen, but a good salesperson understands how precious time is to a client. Upon setting up an appointment, your salesperson is now obligated to keep it and should make every good faith effort to do so. This is one of the most important tasks of a salesperson, and his or her reputation, as well as that of your business, depends on his or her timeliness and reliability.

Checking in with your team member to gauge his or her workload is essential to resolving this issue. If your salesperson is feeling overwhelmed with menial tasks like answering emails, he or she may need additional coaching, assistance in the field, or some time away from the office. As the sales manager, you must remind the salesperson of his or her first responsibility, which is attending to customers to ensure sales are made. Prioritizing any other duty above this one is negligent. These meetings are the setting for sales presentations, persuasion, and sealing deals—without the salesperson, they have no value. Because attending these meetings should be your salesperson's primary objective, I advise offering protected time to complete other tasks as assigned, delegating nonessential tasks to other staff members, and maintaining better communication around workload stress.

2. **Offer training on multitasking—give them juggling lessons!**

Multitasking is the capability to complete more than one task at the same time. I am not a fan of multitasking; I believe it can be an unnecessary distraction and a thief of efficiency. Not everyone agrees with me, however, as multitasking is very much in vogue. Sales is a sink-or-swim industry; this means that in order to swim, you must also learn to multitask. It simply is not possible to avoid other legitimate responsibilities like answering emails. But they should not impede a salesperson's ability to accomplish his or her primary goal. If possible, it may be a good idea to either present some training materials on multitasking or to meet one-on-one to discuss workflow improvement and to develop a plan for how to best accomplish nonsales tasks in a timely manner. The best way to save someone from drowning is to offer a lifeline!

3. **Address sloth in the workplace—don't let them release that beast!**

Sloth is a sneaky beast that can rear its ugly head among your sales team when you're not watching. Research has shown that many employees tend to busy themselves with less important duties at work to avoid completing labor-intensive tasks. Some are busy on their phones all day; others occupy themselves with activities like answering nonessential emails while there is more important work to be done. As a sales manager, you must stop sloth before it takes hold among your sales team. There is a fine line, however, between being a taskmaster and a tyrant. Within reason, allowing your team members to do these less important tasks allows them an opportunity to minimize stress and feel balanced in the workplace. It is still very important, however, to remind them of the company's vision and to regularly review the goals set out for the year. Additionally, reminding them that you are a team and that every member needs to be involved and engaged to reach your goals may also inspire them. Providing recognition and incentives goes a long way in alleviating sloth in the workplace. It may even encourage others to work harder and do a better job of crossing their t's and dotting their i's

4. **Prioritizing—figuring out what really matters**

Prioritizing tasks is essential for every part of life. Setting priorities entails attending to the most demanding situations first while leaving other, less important, issues until later. Teaching your sales team how to prioritize tasks in their workload can be difficult but is of absolute importance if you want to see their best work. Remind them to ask themselves whether each task will help them close a sale or build a customer relationship. If it does not, explore options for how their time could be optimized, and instruct them to complete fewer pressing tasks at another time. If possible, it may be worth demonstrating how you prioritize your own workload, leading by example.

5. **Request a formal apology**

The meeting was missed, and the harm is done; in this situation the best form of damage control is a formal apology. Encourage your team member to write a letter of apology to the client. As the sales manager, however, you may feel more comfortable resolving the issue yourself—especially if you are skillful in this respect. Extending a genuine apology without making too many excuses can be a very effective method of rebuilding customer trust and allowing your business to continue per usual.

Part of being a human being is feeling overwhelmed and occasionally making mistakes. It is a choice, however, to learn from these mistakes. A dedicated, involved team member will respond well to coaching and redirection when it comes from a place of strong leadership, respect, and good intent. A connected, caring manager provides it.

Plan your work and work your plan.
—*Anonymous*

No One Gets Back to Me

Some of the excuses your sales team will give you can be addressed with quick fixes; others require a bit of investigation. For example, if a salesperson comes to you with the complaint that no one replies to place an order, you should acknowledge that this is more of a complaint than an excuse. You will need to spend some time to determine whether this is a personal or professional problem and how best to resolve it. Coaching your team member through this may be a challenge, but by establishing trust, providing constructive feedback, and sharing your own experiences, you can ideally help him or her get the replies he or she needs. I offer the following suggestions for how to approach your salesperson and provide him or her with the needed support:

1. **Shadow your salesperson as he or she works with prospects and customers**

    Observing your salesperson in action will make it easier to understand the problem. This will also provide you with an opportunity to observe his or her presentation style, knowledge of product, and customer service approach and to provide real-time, actionable feedback. He or she may be more open to discussing the situation when you are working side by side. If the issue happens to be personal, you may figure this out during your time together. He or she might feel more comfortable outside the office with your undivided attention in a less formal setting.

    I will caution, however, that this approach may create additional anxiety. Keep your interaction positive and encouraging—offer praise in addition to suggestions for improvement. This will help keep morale up and, hopefully, increase productivity.

2. **Provide support for personal issues**

Personal issues are difficult to address and can range from illnesses to life-altering situations like divorce, the birth of a child, or the death of a family member. You may be empathetic, but don't allow yourself to be manipulated; you still have business objectives to accomplish. Depending on the matter at hand, you may suggest your salesperson take some time off, after which you regularly check in to ensure the issue is resolved. If this will be a long-term issue, additional accommodations may be necessary, including a reduced workload, arranging alternate work solutions (e.g., working from home one day per week), or transfer to another position until he or she is able to return to sales.

3. **Review presentation skills**

If the issue is related to presentation skills, it may be time for a back-to-basics skills review. A good presentation must capture the attention of a potential buyer and be persuasive; ideally, a customer will develop an interest in the product, ask questions, and move toward making a purchase. Provide examples for how best to stimulate dialogue with the customer; sometimes, a simple change or addition to the presentation may be all that's needed to get the customer engaged. For example, I recall a time when one of my sales team members had a difficult time engaging with the customer during a presentation; I suggested that when giving the presentation, the salesperson should give the sample to the customer. By introducing an interactive element, the buyer became a part of the presentation, which immediately changed the direction of the meeting.

4. **Help inspire confidence**

   Sometimes, a good salesperson loses confidence for no specific reason. Instead of pointing out how he or she is not performing well, give reminders them of his or her strengths. Ask your salesperson to recall presentations that went well and what it was that made them successful. Ask your salesperson to recall presentations that were not successful and to suggest how to correct them. It may also be helpful to have your salesperson shadow another strong performing fellow team member to observe his or her approach. Every sales presentation should also be considered a learning opportunity; seeing other ways to make one could help remove your salesperson's mental block.

5. **Give your salesperson an attitude adjustment**

   As a sales manager or small business owner, you may have no problem confronting an underperforming salesperson but find it much more difficult to confront a salesperson with a poor attitude.

   A poor attitude in sales is like a land mine—it is only a matter of time before it affects a relationship with a customer, and it may be the reason that no one is getting back to him or her. Worse, it could also affect the morale of your entire sales team. Therefore, it's imperative to find out the cause. It could be a variety of things, ranging from company policies, to working conditions, to compensation programs, to uncontrollable external factors. Where possible, provide either rationale, a resolution, or support. The solution may not be simple, but showing a good faith effort to making things better for your salesperson where possible will go a long way in developing good interpersonal relationships.

Getting a salesperson back on track can be labor-intensive for both you and your employee. Both of you will have steps to take and work to reach a resolution. Staying open, positive, and communicative with each other will ensure that even if things are not going well, you are committed to helping your salesperson improve. Not every solution will be ideal, and it is likely not everyone will get exactly what he or she wants. If each persons efforts are offered with a willingness to meet the other halfway, a collaborative spirit, and a genuine desire to fix what is wrong, however, the work is half done.

Whatever the mind can conceive and believe the mind can achieve.

—*Napoleon Hill*

My Samples Are Incorrect

I find the excuse of poor or incorrect samples unacceptable. Without question, one of the most important tools in a salesperson's toolbox is a sample collection. To resolve this excuse, the first thing you want to find out is why he or she had a bad or incorrect sample in the first place, especially when the warehouse was filled with the correct product.

People tend to respond most effectively to that which they can see and interact. A product sample is an easy way to provide that experience to a potential buyer. By providing a sample, a salesperson can demonstrate the features and quality of a product that the buyer can then use to judge other items he or she wants to purchase. The concept is very simple: good quality samples encourage sales, confidence, and product loyalty. Poor quality samples do not.

A proper sample is essential to a salesperson because it embodies what customers want after market research and surveys have been conducted. Allowing a customer to view, manipulate, and interact with a sample will often make a better impression than a verbal pitch alone. When one considers that a first impression is often the only impression your salesperson will be allowed to give, the importance of a proper sample is abundantly clear. If your salesperson's sample is bad or incorrect, however, addressing any issue or concern at the beginning of the presentation will not only encourage your customer to trust what your salesperson has to say, but it may potentially stimulate conversations about modifications or improvements the customer would like to see in your company's products.

There are very few instances in which presenting a bad or incorrect sample to a potential buyer may be acceptable, such as if your salesperson has the first generation of a product and is looking for customer input for improvement, or if he or she is attempting to gauge interest in a similar product. A bad or incorrect sample can at least give a customer an idea of how the final product might look or function. Anytime your salesperson presents a less-than-perfect sample, he or she should have a ready explanation for why it is subpar and a plan to either improve upon it or guarantee a better sample in the future. To best prepare your sales force and help them create the best possible presentation, I strongly suggest reviewing proposed samples with them and coaching them through a trial presentation.

One of my salespersons fully understood the need for good, quality samples. We were going to see a customer in Manhattan to sell wheeled luggage. Instead of wheeling the luggage sample in, he picked it up and carried it for three blocks so it wouldn't get dirty or give the buyer an excuse not to pick it up. I tell this story to every salesperson I work with as a testament for keeping samples looking great.

A savvy, quick-thinking salesperson can avoid what could be an embarrassing situation by taking immediate action using the following preventative and corrective measures:

1. **Teamwork makes the dream work—make your sales a team effort**

    Though it is the salesperson's responsibility to bring a correct sample to a presentation, he or she should not be the only one who reviews it. Everyone on a team is bound to make a mistake from time to time—a poor or incorrect sample could have come from the product development department, the sales manager, or the salesperson. The onus falls upon you to help improve the process of developing the best sample possible and then developing a sample distribution policy. For example, a well-documented, numbered inventory may be helpful. When new samples come in, the product development department can assure that they are correct by retrieving the number associated with the prototype, which a salesperson should verify before bringing it to a presentation. When a prototype is no longer in use, it should be destroyed to prevent confusion with other samples.

2. **Know before you go—ensure your samples are correct before your presentation**

   Can you imagine firefighters attempting to extinguish a fire without testing their hoses regularly? A salesperson has a similar responsibility to carefully review samples, ensure they are functional and correct, and have them available to present to a potential client.

3. **Correct and redirect—make things right with your customer**

   Customers usually understand that mistakes will happen and are willing to forgive them if handled correctly. Imagine, for example, upon presenting a sample to the customer, the salesperson discovers the sample is not correct. To salvage the sale, immediate steps must be taken. He or she will need to explain to the customer that the sample is wrong, apologize for the mistake, and attempt to correct the situation. If the correct sample is available in the office, your salesperson should tell the customer the correct sample will be delivered the next day. If the sample is still in final development, he or she must make it clear the client is being heard and that the client's requests will be taken into consideration and incorporated as appropriate. Being attentive and quick to act will show a customer that his or her concerns and opinions are valued and respected, which does a great deal to resolve problems in almost any situation.

As a sales manager or small business owner, you should accept the excuse of a bad or incorrect sample only once. If a member of your sales team repeatedly carries a bad sample into a meeting or cannot recognize a bad or incorrect sample, it is a strong indicator of a lack of attention to detail or dedication to the assignment. Encourage your team to work together to be prepared to meet and exceed your sales goals.

Opportunity does not waste time with those who are unprepared.

—*Idowu Koyenika*

EXCUSE 36
I Do Not Know Why

As I have said before, your job of sales manager or small business owner will feel a bit like being a parent from time to time. If you know or have children, you can understand that nothing is more infuriating than the reply "I don't know" when you ask how something happened. More often than not, children do know, or at the least they know what may have contributed to it. The same is true for a salesperson. When he or she offers this excuse, you should pay close attention to what is *not* being said. There are many reasons why your salesperson may not want to share this information. Perhaps it is a dreaded personal slump. Perhaps it is that your salesperson is not feeling engaged with his or her work. Perhaps external factors are at play. Whatever the reason may be, your salesperson is likely already feeling anxious or ashamed for not meeting his or her goals and will likely be anticipating some sort of intervention from a supervisor. As a manager, you may have an undeniable urge to respond to this excuse with something like, "I'm sure you know why if you think about it." However, this type of response could put your employee on the defense and close a conversation before it ever takes place. Instead, consider some of the following tactics to allow your salesperson to open up to you and help you both get to the heart of the issue:

1. **Ask open-ended questions**

   The best starting point to finding an answer to this problem is to ask open-ended, feelings-based questions to stimulate a conversation. For example, you may begin with an observation and then follow it up with a question about the issue without sounding accusatory. Allow your salesperson time to process both your question and his or her response. Then, listen closely to what you are being told. Allow this employee the opportunity to feel that he or she can trust you. Look for cues for follow-up questions to gather additional information.

"Sarah, I've noticed that you haven't met your goal this month. Can you tell me about what is happening for you?"

Because she's been asked a question that requires more than a yes or no reply, Sarah will have to give additional thought to it, and more information may come forth as a result. Yes-or-no questions can easily end a conversation—don't allow this to happen if you are truly interested in the answer.

2. **Listen without judgment. Think before you reply.**

Remember, this is about the salesperson and his or her reply. Your job is to consider what is said and the feelings of the person saying them and to reflect on that before adding your own opinions into the mix.

For example, let's say Sarah replies, "I'm having a hard time meeting my goals this month because I've got a lot going on in my personal life. I'm feeling a lot of stress."

You might be tempted to ask additional questions about the source of her stress, but it is important to first ask yourself whether those answers will help resolve the situation. If so, be prepared—your team member may not be willing to share this information, so focus on the feelings she does share to keep the conversation flowing. An appropriate response could be to say, "I'm sorry you're experiencing that. Is there anything I can do here that could help?"

If attempting to offer a solution, make sure the offer is both genuine and something that can be done, whether it's a day off, a space to talk, or a cup of coffee. Perhaps further intervention is required. Follow the lead of your salesperson and continue to look for clues.

3. **Strategize together about how to get back on track**

   You likely know your staff well. You understand what it takes to keep them engaged and inspired, how they work under pressure, and how to motivate them when they're not optimally performing. Again, ask your salesperson open-ended questions to determine what success might look like for his or her at this time and how he or she might achieve it. Consider whether your salesperson is feeling valued and appreciated. Does he or she have any incentive to work harder? What is an ideal incentive for this salesperson? What, if anything, can you offer? It bears repeating that if you offer an incentive, make sure that you can deliver it.

4. **Follow up and check in until the problem are resolved**

   As the saying goes, "Rome wasn't built in a day." The same is true for rebuilding confidence and trust and for adjusting or taking corrective action. Be patient, within reason, but assure your salesperson that you have heard what he or she has to say, that you understand his or her position, and that you are available for additional support. Then check in regularly to determine whether further actions are required.

Getting to the bottom of a nebulous excuse like "I don't know" will require time and understanding. Don't let frustration and impatience block the channels of communication because they will be difficult to reopen. Instead, consider the times you've doubted your own abilities— did you feel heard? Did you have leadership who treated you with honesty and respect? How did the issue resolve for you? By looking inward and employing "the golden rule," you may find tools to help get the answers you seek.

Goals without a plan is just a wish.
—*Antoine de Saint-Exupery*

CONCLUSION

Now that you've read these excuses and my suggestions for resolving them, many may seem familiar or easily relatable. The objective of this book is to provide you with solutions you can implement to mitigate excuses for not getting the order so your team can become more productive and increase sales. In addition, you can take several other steps that will not cost money but will require your time and a strong desire:

1. **A sales information book**

   This will be an ongoing book as objections and excuses come up. In section 1, I said that many excuses could be mitigated if you have a sales information book that specifies what your company is about, its goals, and its challenges. You need to be open to receiving information about negative customer experiences and explaining how problems have been corrected. Discuss details of your quality standards and how they compare to competitors' standards or to your company's past standards. Also include details about your terms and conditions. You can continue to add new objections that come up. This will give you a place to explain before an excuse for not getting the order becomes a repeated problem.

2. **Coaching**

   Coaching is essential for your entire sales team, including your best salespersons. Even they will need coaching from time to time, just like professional ball players do. Coaching should be a continuous process that can easily be incorporated into a regular sales team meeting. If you're not doing so already, you should be meeting with your team at least once a month. Coaching can take as little as five minutes, but it should be done regularly.

Yes, time is a problem, and it will always be a problem, but you need to remember that sales is the "oxygen in your business blood stream." Bring up some of the objections that you have heard, including any new ones. Review them collectively to come up with logical responses.

It is a good idea for your sales support team to be part of the regular sales meeting; they should be given the same information as your salespersons. Too often, sales teams meet without the sales support staff, who also face similar objections and ought to be included as part of the team. As with any coaching, some of your employees will need to be coached on a one-on-one basis. The salespeople with weak excuses from section 3 will have to be coached on regular basis to see if they can remain part of the team.

3. **Monitoring**

You need to monitor each of your salespeople to see if he or she is repeating excuses or coming up with new ones. Are your salesperson's sales increasing, decreasing, or staying stagnant? Over time, monitoring will help you rate your salespeople, determine the weakest, and either put them in another position or terminate them. Making these decisions is difficult, but you are not doing them any good by keeping them employed in a position that they cannot or do not want to do. The majority of salespeople that I terminated found another position with a company that better fit their talents.

If you continually implement these methods, you will see a reduction in excuses and an increase in sales. Try it for three months and review your results. I would like to know how it works for you. You can write me at Thomas@thomasmartucci.com.

ABOUT THE AUTHOR

Thomas Martucci not only loves sales; he is passionate about it! He writes, speaks, coaches, and gives seminars to small business owners and sales managers for small companies. He helps make salespeople and their management teams much more productive. With more than twenty-five years as a business owner selling consumer goods and ten years with mid-to-large companies in sales and senior sales management roles, he has the experience and know-how to make things happen. Salespeople who have worked alongside him and his competitors call him a true road warrior because he has been on the road and in the trenches, working diligently to get orders.

He has lived the problems and frustrations with sales, cash flow, and administration in his own company. As a sales manager and senior sales manager for mid-to-large companies, he understands the frustrations of managing both independent sales agents and an in-house sales team.

He can "talk the walk" because he has "walked the talk" in real life. He shares these experiences in the book *The Excuse Department Is Closed.*

www.ingramcontent.com/pod-product-compliance
Lightning Source LLC
Chambersburg PA
CBHW021414210526
45463CB00001B/366